Thanks for reading,

Blake Sebring

Legends of the Komets

By Blake Sebring

authorHOUSE®

AuthorHouse™
1663 Liberty Drive, Suite 200
Bloomington, IN 47403
www.authorhouse.com
Phone: 1-800-839-8640

First published by AuthorHouse 1/6/2009

ISBN: 978-1-4389-4275-9 (sc)

Printed in the United States of America
Bloomington, Indiana

This book is printed on acid-free paper.

DEDICATION

This is for Pam and Jim Wallace who have always believed and provided encouragement.

Thanks to Ruth Weigmann, Sheryl Krieg, Betty Stein, Chuck Bailey, Ed Rose, George Drysdale and the most important people of all to the Komets legends, their wives who put up with my constant phone calls.

Cover photo by Aaron Suozzi of The News-Sentinel, Jan. 9, 2004, used with permission.

Interior photos courtesy of the Fort Wayne Komets and The News-Sentinel, used with permission.

FOREWARD

For 56 years the Fort Wayne Komets have been a vibrant example of what is good about our city. In the late 1940s the idea of the Memorial Coliseum created tremendous dreams about what could become reality in Fort Wayne, Indiana. The new building brought about the Zollner Pistons and the Fort Wayne Komets. As history played out, it was the Komets, who were actually the second sports team in the coliseum that made it long-term. The Pistons are long gone to Detroit, but the Fort Wayne Komets have remained as an institution in Fort Wayne.

Generations of Komets fans have come and gone in 56 years to make Fort Wayne one of the best minor league hockey cities in North America. It is that fan base that has made the Fort Wayne Komets a model franchise in all of minor league sports. This organization belongs to Fort Wayne, and as owners we are merely keepers of this franchise. To the many Komets fans who will read this book, we can only say thank you for your support of this team.

For many of you, it started back in the 1950s, coming to Komet games with your family. Now you attend with your children and grandchildren. For others, it was the championships of the 1960s, 1970s, 1990s or of the new century that started your love affair. With the Komets, as the song said, "The beat goes on," and for the Komets and their fans it's never sounded better.

The Komet players have been a huge part of the team's success in Fort Wayne. The numbers of former Komets living in Fort Wayne today is staggering; a true testament to what our city is all about. It's wonderful to know that George Drysdale, the first Komets' elected captain, has lived almost his entire adult life in Fort Wayne, working and raising his family here. Now retired, you'll find George at Komet games working as an off-ice official as he has a true love for the Komet organization and this city.

Retiring jersey numbers of long-time Komet players is a tradition in Fort Wayne. For a number of years that tradition was broken, but in the early 1990s we decided it was time to re-institute the retired numbers. For many of us growing up in the 1960s and 1970s, the names of Thornson, Repka, Long, Primeau, Irons and Pembroke were our idols as fans. Today their numbers are retired to the rafters of the coliseum. Later the names of Chin, Chase, Fletcher, Laird, Ullyot, Lister and Gallmeier were hoisted to the rafters.

Many times fans have asked us how we determine who gets to have their name retired into the history of Komets hockey. The answer is simple, longevity, accomplishments and the intangibles of making a difference for this organization go into the entire process of choosing. All of these men passed the test with flying colors.

Will others follow? Yes, in due time there will be others, but the names and numbers will become less as time moves on because everything is different today. Players don't stay in one place like they used to. It's a different world we live in today... even in the hockey world.

Which makes you appreciate even more what these men have accomplished and meant to the Komets. Enjoy!

Michael and David Franke

KOMETS HOCKEY 1962-63 SEASON   25c

EDDIE LONG

CHAPTER 1

During his 43 years as the sports editor of The News-Sentinel, Ben Tenny wrote one hockey story. He was a basketball guy first, second and last, but even he could appreciate something special on a rink when he saw it.

Before the Fort Wayne Komets started play in 1952, they hosted an exhibition to explain the rules and strategy to a new group of fans. One Komet in particular caught Tenny's eye.

``It didn't take me long to see that the young short skater who was wearing No. 16 on his white jersey had that desire to win and get ahead that makes some athletes outstanding," Tenny wrote. ``If the play of this youngster is typical of the play fans will see in the International Hockey League, hockey will make it in Fort Wayne."

It could be argued that Long might have been the most important player in Komets history. As much as anyone, he gave the Komets their identity. Particularly at the start, Long's hustle, grit and ability were something that attracted new fans to the team and the game. Then he maintained that excellence during a 14-year career and finished as the IHL's all-time leading scorer.

``But Eddie Long is more than a statistic – he's the spirit of competition," Bud Gallmeier wrote at Long's retirement in 1965. ``He only knew one way to play the game – as hard as he could. Eddie would burn more energy during one shift on the ice than many players do in an entire game."

That's also the way Long has lived his life.

Eddie Long was born June 11, 1933, the fifth of five children for Gus and Tootie Long in Ottawa, Ontario. Gus was a captain in the

Canadian Army for 33 years, and Tootie ran a boarding house. There was an ice rink next to the house, but that was about the only thing that was easy about Long's early life. His two older brothers, Brady and Harry, were killed during World War II.

Brady was married, had one child and another on the way, but he kept pestering his father to pull some strings so he could fight in Europe. He was sailing on a ship from Halifax when disaster struck.

``They are just about over there, and the air planes that are scouting say everything is OK, but they miss this one sub," Eddie said. ``It was 10:30 p.m. and they got hit with five torpedoes and he drowned."

Harry, who had joined the RAF, was waiting for Brady in Europe at the time. He later joined the Royal Canadian Air Force and was shot down in February 1944.

``I remember it was a Sunday afternoon, and I was outside playing," Long said. ``I saw this car come up to the house, and I went in the house and I saw my mom and dad crying. My dad just said, 'Go on out and play hockey.' I came back in and looked at the telegram. It said, 'Your son is missing in action/presumed dead.'

``My mother and father went through a lot. From that moment on, my dad was actually dead but alive. Then, when I came to Fort Wayne, it was like the good Lord gave him another chance at life. I really didn't have a father, not that he neglected me in any way, but he was hurting so much."

The Longs lived in a district called Sandy Hill and it had an overabundance of future NHL players, most of whom started playing on the rink Long's father had built and flooded every night. It measured 100 feet long by 25 feet wide. Eddie had started skating when he was 1 year old.

They called it the ``Our Gang Hockey League" and it was made up of about six teams with nine players each from the neighborhood.

Long didn't play official organized hockey until he was 12 in the Ottawa Boys League, and then he finished first in scoring. Because of the accomplishment, he was presented a knife by Toronto Maple Leaf great King Clancy.

``He was going to bring me a hockey stick, but I didn't pursue it," Long said.

Then he played bantam hockey followed by midget and juvenile. He went to a Catholic high school at age 13. Luckily it was on an athletic scholarship because Long never cared much for his studies. In fact, he quit school at age 17 to work in Army ordinance.

He was also an accomplished baseball pitcher.

``If I had lived down here (in the United States) I probably would have pursued baseball," he said. ``I wasn't fast, but I had a lot of stuff on the ball. I was the youngest guy in the league and my record was 7-1 when I pitched. But hockey was my sport. I was more mentally geared for hockey."

But the baseball tie helped in an odd way. When Alex Wood was named coach of the expansion Fort Wayne Komets in 1952 after winning a pair of Turner Cups with Toledo, he returned to Ottawa where he used to coach and asked some of his former players who some of the hot talent was. Some of Long's baseball teammates had played for Wood before and suggested the scrappy right wing.

``He came to the front door and came into the house and talked to my dad and me and offered me a contract," Long said. ``That's how I came to Fort Wayne."

Actually, he almost didn't get to Fort Wayne. Training camp that year was in Woodstock, Ontario, and Long was not impressed when he arrived.

``I asked them where the coach was and I went up to the room and all these guys are sitting around having a few beers and smoking," Long said. ``That was quite a shock for 19-year-old kid. I came down and just said I'm going back home. I'm sitting in the lobby and Dougy Houston comes down and introduces himself and says, `I'm going to room with you.' I tell him it doesn't look too good here and I'm going

3

to go home. He says, 'Look, you have to remember one thing, Eddie. These guys aren't going to feel too good in the morning when they have to go out on the ice.' "

Especially after they ran into the hungry rookie who didn't mind dropping the gloves when necessary.

Wood had been a goaltender in the American Hockey League who got one National Hockey League game with the New York Americans in 1937. He put together a scrappy team in Fort Wayne to set the tone for the Komets squads of the future.

``I think Alex should be recognized," Long said. ``He only coached here one year, but he set the precedent as far as the everyday player of what we had. We had an entertaining team. He didn't direct you too much. One guy said, 'I'm thinking coach...,' and he said, 'Don't. You'll screw the whole team up.' The point is, just go out and play the game."

That first season was a bit rocky for the Komets. No one at Memorial Coliseum knew how to flood the ice, the uniforms were white with maroon numbers and the public address announcer, who was co-owner Ramon Perry, started another Fort Wayne tradition by editorializing a bit before being removed from the job.

``I got $95 a week, and for the first month I had headaches after every game and they didn't know what was wrong with me," Long said. ``This was the first time I had played in a heated rink, and it took me a while to adjust."

Long scored 31 goals and 52 points that first season in 60 games as the Komets finished 20-38-2. For some reason they gave the perennial champion Cincinnati Mohawks fits. The Mohawks lost only 13 games that season, but six of the losses were to the Komets.

Before the next season, Long attended training camp with the AHL's Buffalo Bison, but he really never had a shot.

``Gaye Stewart was the coach and he said, 'This is my last year in hockey, Eddie, it's such a big clique it's pathetic,' " Long said. ``This guy played 14 years in the NHL. He said, 'You are better than half the guys out there, but they are not going to keep you, you've got nobody backing you.' I decided I'm going back to Fort Wayne and playing as long as I can. I'm not moving."

One of the players he met at that training camp was future Komet teammate Hartley McLeod.

Unfortunately, the Komets lost a lot of their team unity over the next few seasons, mostly because they kept changing coaches. Long wasn't happy, scoring 15 goals during his second season.

``That was the worst year I ever had in hockey," he said. ``If I was going to quit, I'd have quit then. It's the only year I never got 20 goals. I got a concussion when Doug McCaig hit me with a good clean check, and I think I was getting stitches every game.

``It really became more of an individual game. You had to produce, and not that you wouldn't pass the puck but it was a matter of survival. You go to training camp, and some of these guys are putting on weight!"

Because he was only about 5-8, 165 pounds, he earned the nickname ``Tiny Mite," and because of that nickname his line of Art Stone and Edgar Blondin the next season were known as the ``Mighty Mites," the first Fort Wayne line to earn a nickname. Stone and Blondin were also listed at 5-8, and that line became the primary focus of Komet fans.

Long had solid offensive years, but he wasn't getting much help. He was known as much for his fighting as he was his overall skills. He wouldn't take any crap from anybody, and it didn't matter how big they were. He started the trend of scrappy smaller players the Komets continued over the years with players such as Robbie Laird, Andy Bezeau and Bruce Richardson.

``They couldn't knock him down, and I don't ever remember him being on the bottom of the pile," long-time Komets coach, general manager and owner Ken Ullyot said.

One thing really kept Long from being miserable during the times when the Komets struggled early in their existence. When he was home in Ottawa, Long used to eat supper at home and then walk over to eat again the house of buddies Neil and Mike Buchanan, who became the first twins to play for the Komets. Fort Wayne girl Beverly Michelle was dating Neil Buchanan and met Long in the summer of 1954.

``One night I'm at the Berghoff Gardens and she walks by and I say `hi'," Long said. ``We start talking and she asks how I'm doing and I say, `I can't find any girls to take out in this town.' I'm joking, see, but she said, `I'll fix you up with my little sister.' It was a Tuesday night when I met Gayle, I think I got a couple of stitches that night and I met her after the game on a blind date."

The stitches were actually on his lip.

``I knew I didn't have to worry about getting a kiss from him that night," Gayle said, laughing.

The date was November 16, 1954. He was 21 and she was 18 and recently graduated from Central Catholic. They were married June 30, 1956 at St. Jude's and started their own team almost immediately. Valerie was born April 6, 1957; Brady on May 21, 1958; Michelle on March 23, 1961; Kristine on Aug. 25, 1962; Theresa on Dec. 14, 1964; and Kathy on May 20, 1965.

``Meeting Gayle is the reason I stayed here because I was ready to go home to Ottawa," Long said.

His parents loved Gayle, particularly his father who enjoyed visiting Fort Wayne and sometimes talking with Bob Chase on WOWO between periods. Besides listening to the games on radio, he also subscribed to The News-Sentinel so he could follow Eddie's exploits and track the statistics.

``He also played for a long time on Army teams and was still playing until he was 48, which is amazing because my dad was only 5-6 and 135 pounds soaking wet, but he had great stature," Eddie said.

Long also provided the question and answer for a trivia contest in the spring of 1958 when he played one playoff game with Louisville. The Rebels ran out of players and needed an emergency fill-in. Long scored a goal in his one game.

The Komets outlook started to change in the summer of 1958 when Ken Ullyot was hired to coach the team. Until then, the Komets had not produced a winning season or won a playoff series. The team had lost $87,000 during the 1957-58 season. Everyone took a pay cut including Long who went from $150 a week to $100. Even training camp was held in Troy that season to save money.

``That first year he came in, I just about didn't make the team," Long said. ``I can see his point of why he'd want to clean house from the standpoint that he didn't want anybody second-guessing him. He was making the point that he was running the show, which I liked. We finally had some organization. You could see Ken knew what he had to do to have a contending team.

``You could see that we had a nucleus over the years, but we needed direction and guys who were committed. We needed somebody to come in and show us some more basics of hockey, which he did. He made us think."

And Long thrived under Ullyot's system scoring 33, 44, 34, 48 and 56 goals over the next five seasons. He was named the IHL's Most Valuable Player in 1963 after putting up a career-high 56 goals and 102 points. During that season he scored 48 goals in the Komets' first 48 games.

``He was a hard worker," Ullyot said. ``If it did not work the first time he'd made it the second time. You could see the determination. He was always thinking, `Somebody's going to take my job.' He was always a bouncing ball.''

But there were times when Ullyot used Long as an example.

"If you stunk the period out and didn't do too well and I thought you could do better, I'd go in and give Eddie hell because maybe you couldn't take it," Ullyot said. ``You'd get worse if I criticized you."

Long remembers those times vividly.

``There was one night in Louisville where I've got a goal or two, but we're playing just terrible," Long said. ``In the locker room between periods, Ken jumps all over me, and it ticked me off. I was taught by my parents that you respect your elders no matter what the situation and this was not the time to go after him. Anyway, at the end of the year just before the party I went up to him. 'What did you jump all over me that night in Louisville for?' He said, 'You were the only guy working out there.' I said, 'Thank you for the honest answer and have a good evening.' He just knew how to do things like that."

Things all came together for the Komets in 1959-60 as Long scored 44 goals and 88 points and the team dominated the regular season. Then came the heartbreaking Game 4 finals loss to St. Paul in four overtimes. A key play in the game was Len Ronson missing a penalty shot on Saints' goaltender Glenn Ramsay.

``That was when you could designate who could take the shot, and Ken and I discussed it," Long said. ``Ken wanted me to take it because I could beat Ramsay nine times out of 10 and Ramsay knew it, but again we're getting back to being a team and we had a guy who had just set the league record with 62 goals. He's got two goals in the game so what do you do? Do you go against the odds? But he lost the puck at the end."

And the Komets lost the game and the series.

``After we got beat that seventh game on a Monday night, everybody was crying," Long said. ``We had one h--- of a hockey team, and we just got beat. We really lost the Turner Cup in that overtime game."

They also lost players like John Ferguson, Andy Voykin, Duane Rupp and Ronson, meaning they had to reload. They added Lloyd Maxfield, Roger Maisonneuve, Chuck Adamson and Bobby Rivard before the 1962-63 season to set up an epic playoff run.

The key game in the postseason that year was Game 6 of the semifinals against Muskegon. The Komets trailed 6-1 before rallying to tie the game behind five assists from Long, but it was a defensive play that saved the game in overtime that will be remembered forever. Muskegon's Larry Lund blasted a shot on Adamson from 10 feet out, which Adamson blocked but the puck went through his legs and trickled toward the goal line. It was halfway across when Long popped into the crease to slap the puck away.

``I'll never know why I turned back in," Long said. ``We had possession of the puck. It was just one of those amazing things. Then I saw the puck and started cutting back in. It was like somebody pushed me that way. It was an amazing thing."

The Komets eventually won in overtime and later crushed Minneapolis to win their first Turner Cup. Long finished with 20 points in 11 playoff games. After coming close a handful of times, the Komets were finally champions.

``The longer you go and you don't win, the harder it is because you have to start all over again from Game 1 the next year," Long said. ``It was so frustrating, and then you'd get nervous when you got close. When it was all over with, it was really a matter of we'd finally won it."

Throughout his career, Long always had excellent playoff statistics, in part, he said, because he treated every shift as if it could be his last one.

``He was real hard-working," Reggie Primeau said. ``I missed the first part, so he didn't fight a lot. I know he did earlier, but he was still mean but he wasn't dirty. He was a real digger. He always worked hard."

Long came back for one more full season in 1963-64, scoring 27 goals and 68 points and announcing his retirement. The Komets had an ``Eddie Long Night" on March 27, 1964, giving him a recliner, a freezer with food in it and a color TV. It was about $5,000 worth of prizes including about $900 in checks from the fans. The league also presented Long with a personalized clock.

Only two athletes in Fort Wayne history have ever had individual nights, Curley Armstrong and Eddie Long.

It turned out to be a partial retirement. Long went behind the Komets' bench to start the 1964-65 season and ended up playing 38 games and scoring 30 points. Whenever the team had too many injuries or needed a spark, he'd suit up. The Komets won their second Turner Cup that spring.

Long coached the next season, playing in 20 more games, before retiring for good. Nagging injuries forced him off the ice at the age of 32.

He finished his Komets career with 459 goals, 465 assists and 924 points while earning 845 penalty minutes in 858 games. He ranks second in games played, goals, assists and points and is ninth in penalty minutes on the franchise's all-time lists. When the Komets opened their Hall of Fame in 1988, he was the first inductee.

After leaving the Komets, Long ran ``This Old House" restaurant for a year. He had worked for AALCO Distributing during the summers since 1957 and joined the company full-time in 1966. He retired at age 67 in March 2001 after 25 years as the sales manager. Now his time is partly occupied by 13 grandchildren and one great-grandchild.

But just because he retired didn't mean ``Steady Eddie" was done working or playing.

Though he's in his 70s, Long is still playing, now in the non-hitting "Old Guys Hockey League" for players age 40 and older on Sunday afternoons at Memorial Coliseum. He's the oldest player in the league by 10 years, even though when he was 57 he said he'd retire at 60.

"He's doing what he loves and it keeps him healthy," Gayle said in 2005. "I'm real proud of him, and I'm his best fan. The last time he said he was going to quit was at 65, but I never mentioned it, and he kept signing up."

He had a good excuse to quit at 65, too, with his left hip being replaced, but he was ready to go when the season started five months later, telling everyone it hurt less to skate than it did to walk. Now his doctor says his hip is postcard perfect.

"He has the muscle tone and the bone structure of someone who is 40 years younger," said Dr. William Berghoff, an orthopedic surgeon at Orthopedics Northeast who specializes in arthritis of the hip and knee. "He comes out of an era with a work ethic and values that every day you get out and you do everything you can, stay in shape, work hard and live a good life. Retirement and Eddie Long is an oxymoron."

During the games, which are played without intermissions and have few stoppages, the only concession Long makes to his age is sticking near the center-ice red line most of the time on defense, making it easier to skate back into the offensive zone. His stride is a tad slower than it is in everyone's memories, but he can still make the moves, often laying out backhand passes with his straight stick and heading directly to the net for rebounds.

"I just think he's a lot of inspiration," said former IHL player Bruce McKay, 45. "When I'm his age, I hope I have that attitude. I just wish there were more Eddie Longs out there."

He's the only player on the ice, maybe in the state, who uses a straight stick. He ordered a batch in the mid-1990s through the Komets.

Every once in a while, Long gets a burst of energy and shows he can still handle the puck, is still strong enough to use his body to keep it away from defenders and still knows all the game's tricks. When he gets going, the players call it a "'50s flashback."

"He's really another one of those gifts from God," his son Brady said. "I'm out there skating sometimes and it's almost like a virtual reality trip. How many kids would just love to still be playing with their dad, and I still get to go out there and play hockey with him every Sunday."

``I don't know how guys can just completely forget about it," Eddie said. ``I just don't know how they can do that. I never really got out of it."

It also doesn't hurt that he sometimes gets to play with his grandson Andy.

Because of who he was and continues to be, Long might have been the most important Komets player and the most recognizable one, as well. He was the star play the fans identified with during its first years when it was fighting for stability. He still gets frequent requests to sign autographs more than 40 years after his playing days.

``Another thing that makes Fort Wayne great is that the people make the players; the players don't make the people," he said.

Though he never has, if he ever got too big a head, Gayle would let him have it.

``I never saw him with his chest puffed up," he said. ``I get a big kick out of people wanting autographs from him. It's nice, but it's not important to him and maybe that's why he enjoys it. We always had kids in the neighborhood stopping by to see if they could get a stick from him. I thought it was great that the kids felt they could do that."

He truly was and is ``Mr. Komet."

``What more can you contribute to hockey than Eddie did?" Ullyot asked. ``He gave his life to the game in Fort Wayne."

Coaching

Season	Team	League	GP	W-L-T	Pts	Playoffs
64-65	Fort Wayne	IHL	70	40-25-5	85	won Turner Cup
65-66	Fort Wayne	IHL	70	38-26-6	82	lost in semi-finals

Season	Team	League	GP	G	A	PTS	PIM	GP	G	A	PTS	PIM
52-53	Fort Wayne	IHL	60	31	21	52	46	*	*	*	*	*
53-54	Fort Wayne	IHL	62	23	19	42	45	2	0	1	1	0
54-55	Fort Wayne	IHL	54	15	23	38	69	*	*	*	*	*
55-56	Fort Wayne	IHL	60	27	32	59	47	4	1	0	1	0
56-57	Fort Wayne	IHL	58	34	25	59	40	*	*	*	*	*
57-58	Fort Wayne	IHL	64	38	21	59	59	4	1	1	2	0
57-58	Louisville	IHL	*	*	*	*	*	1	1	0	1	0
58-59	Fort Wayne	IHL	56	33	34	67	61	11	11	6	17	32
59-60	Fort Wayne	IHL	67	44	44	88	63	13	6	6	12	11
60-61	Fort Wayne	IHL	69	45	29	74	42	8	2	4	6	8
61-62	Fort Wayne	IHL	58	48	48	96	106	*	*	*	*	*
62-63	Fort Wayne	IHL	70	56	46	102	44	11	5	15	20	7
63-64	Fort Wayne	IHL	65	27	41	68	67	12	5	4	9	9
64-65	Fort Wayne	IHL	38	9	21	30	16	*	*	*	*	*
65-66	Fort Wayne	IHL	20	6	5	11	20	*	*	*	*	*

BOB CHASE

CHAPTER 2

Before broadcasting the 1992 International Hockey League All-Star Game in Atlanta, Bob Chase was setting up his equipment when he looked up to see the stare of an older gentleman of diminutive stature. The man stood there for several seconds.

``Can I help you?" Chase asked.

``Nope," the man said. ``You Bob Chase?"

After getting a positive nod, the man immediately left, only to reappear five minutes later with a female companion, obviously his wife.

``See," the man said, pointing, ``that's what he looks like."

And then they left.

There are a million similar stories. Other than General Mad Anthony Wayne, it's likely no one has represented or been more associated with Fort Wayne on a national level than Bob Chase. The strange thing is, at first Chase didn't really want to come to the Summit City.

After coming home from four years in the Navy, Chase was majoring in accounting and minoring in psychology and speech at Marquette's Northern Michigan University in 1951. He was waiting for a promised job to open up with the Clifford Cliffs Iron Company where he was going to set up an economic education program to help the miners who, at the time, were on strike.

But the strike went on and the job never materialized so Chase was working at radio station, WDMJ. Besides broadcasting Marquette Sentinels hockey games, he also pulled a regular shift reading the news. A friend was getting married in Marquette one Saturday, but Chase had to run back to the station for a newscast before the reception. On her way to the reception, the groom's aunt heard his broadcast and was impressed so she called good friend and WOWO program manager Guy Harris to recommend Chase when she returned home.

``Mr. Harris called me and wanted to know if I could send him a tape," Chase said. ``I didn't pay much attention to him because I had never intended to go into the broadcasting business as a career. A week goes by and I'm doing a show when the phone rings. This voice says, `Where the hell is that tape?' I told him I mailed the tape yesterday, so then I taped what I was doing that day and mailed it. A few days later he calls me up and wants me to come down."

Chase enjoyed his work but never figured radio would become his career. Harris convinced him otherwise.

Another irony is that Chase was hired as a general on-air announcer and not as a sports broadcaster. WOWO already had Ernie Ashley as sports director, and he called the Komets' games during their inaugural season. Only after Chase arrived did WOWO officials find out he had an interest in sports.

The station set him up as Ashley's color man for the home hockey games, and he would fill in on play-by-play whenever Ashley was late coming back from covering Saturday afternoon Big Ten games.

``I would do the games, and Ernie would come racing back from Bloomington, run into the coliseum and just flat grab the mike from me and start going," Chase said. ``He felt threatened, I guess. They thought he was a hockey guy because he was from Minnesota, but he wasn't."

Maybe he did feel the heat because by January Ashley had left to take a job as a station manager in Louisville, leaving the Komets and Fort Wayne to Chase. Now, it's hard to imagine they were ever separated. Of the more than 4,500 games the Komets have played in 56 years, Chase has called at least 4,000 of them. He's lasted longer with one team than any other sports broadcaster with the exception of Foster Hewitt with the Toronto Maple Leafs. Chase will break Hewitt's mark with his 56th season in 2007-08.

Everyone else is in awe of Chase's accomplishments, but he's in awe of his audience.

``Had it not been for the public who accepted me, I wouldn't be here,'' Chase said. ``Whenever you are in my business, if the radio is on and they are listening, it's by invitation only because the minute they don't like you, they are on to something else.''

During his early life, it always seemed like Chase was moving onto something else as he tried a little bit of everything. He was born Robert Donald Wallenstein on January 22, 1926 in Negaunee, Michigan, on the Upper Peninsula. He grew up playing football, hockey and baseball in the Upper Peninsula, rooting for the Red Wings, Lions and Tigers. His favorite sport was baseball where he was a pitcher and first baseman.

After graduating high school, Wallenstein enlisted in the Navy at age 17 to become a pilot, but his height of six feet, six inches became a problem because he couldn't fit in the cockpit of most planes. He later became part of a code-monitoring team in Hawaii.

He came home in December 1946, and started dating Muriel ``Murph'' Chase, who was a student nurse. They met when Bob went to visit his mother who was a special-duty nurse at the hospital in Marquette. Appropriately, on their first date he took her to watch a hockey game. He didn't think they'd make it past that night.

``I took her home and went to give her a goodnight kiss and (she moved) and pecked her right on the top of the nose,'' he said. ``I figured that was it, I'd blown it and she'd never want to go out with me again. I've improved a little bit since then.''

They were married April 6, 1950 and now have three sons, a daughter and seven grandchildren.

``Murph has never missed a hockey game to my knowledge since she has come to Fort Wayne,'' Bob said. ``Only a handful of times in all my years of broadcasting have I been able to coerce her into going into the press box and sitting while I am doing a game. She just doesn't feel like she should do that. She's always there, and whatever time the bus comes home in the morning, the door's unlocked and she's always there for me.''

Because of his time in the service, Chase was 27 by the time he came to Fort Wayne. Harris thought Wallenstein was too long and encouraged a name change. Bob picked Chase to honor Murph's father whom he was very close to. The man had fathered five daughters but no sons, and now someone would carry on his name. No one knew how far it would carry as the International Hockey League and WOWO's signal continued to grow.

``The league at that time was a homey little thing," he said. ``Mostly the guys were players who couldn't make it in the NHL and had nowhere to play. If they were going to make $75, $80 a week, they might as well make it in Fort Wayne as up there where the snow was 10 feet deep. When this league got under way, there were some great hockey players. The talent was incredible, and I enjoyed it."

After Ashley left, Chase took over the Komets and also became WOWO's sports director. Oddly, during the early days the first period was blacked out on the home games, fearing it would hurt the attraction for paying customers. Then for a while the road games were cut back, but by 1964 all the road games were broadcast and shortly after that the home games could be heard in their entirety.

``We had 12 skaters and one goaltender and the trainer would be the back-up goaltender," Chase said. ``We'd travel in three or four cars all the way to Johnstown, Pennsylvania, Denver, Milwaukee or wherever. You'd shop around for hotels that would give you $3.50 a night double-occupancy. Those were the days when breakfast cost 85 or 90 cents and a steak dinner cost $3. You could almost make it, and everybody was having fun."

In 1958, the Komets almost left WOWO and Chase. The team announced losses of $87,000 at the end of the 1957-58 season and was looking for any possible revenue source. After the NBA's Fort Wayne Pistons left for Detroit in 1957, WKJG Radio and Hilliard Gates offered the Komets $50 per game.

``We almost lost it right there," Chase said. ``We just finally prevailed when we proved to them that the signal WKJG had would not have served their market."

The Komets once left WOWO in 1985-86 for WBTU, keeping Chase as their announcer, but came back the next season. There were other times when Chase had to fight to keep the Komets on the air.

``It got to the point one time that the sales manager said, `Look, I'm not taking my salespeople and wasting their time trying to sell sports,' '' Chase said. ``So one time I went out and in about four days had about $50,000 sold, and then he was really mad because I was interfering with his salespeople.''

The Komets started in Fort Wayne in 1952, shortly after WOWO increased its strength from 10,000 to 50,000 watts. That signal carried Chase and the Komets over the eastern half of the United States and well into Canada. Players liked it because their parents could listen to the games. Chase's popularity grew so much that some players said they couldn't wait to be interviewed by him, and several asked relatives to record the interviews for keepsakes. Even opponents regularly asked Chase to say hi to their folks during games.

``Bob used to say hello to my parents back in Boston whenever we played Fort Wayne,'' Olympic gold medalist Mike Eruzione said. ``WOWO was the only station that my family could listen to a few games on. Bob has not only dedicated his life to the sport as an announcer, but he has also become a great ambassador of U.S. hockey, always being there for the players and their families.''

Chase once joked that WOWO's signal was so strong that Santa Claus probably listened to most of the games. Because of the signal and his passion, Chase's fame continued to spread. It was common for Fort Wayne natives wearing Komets apparel visiting other cities to be asked about Chase. One time Chase was eating lunch with friends in a Louisville restaurant when someone overheard the familiar voice and came to the table. ``OK, which one of you is Bob Chase?''

Besides the Komets, Chase worked the Indianapolis 500 for 35 years, and also broadcast Big Ten football games, flying back to Fort Wayne in time for the Saturday night hockey games. He went to the Rose Bowl with Indiana in 1968, and in 1954 broadcast the 1954 Milan-

Muncie Central state championship basketball game that became the basis for the movie ``Hoosiers.''

``At the time, I didn't think I was witnessing anything of unbelievable importance,'' Chase said. ``The thing I remember most is trying to fill the time while Milan held the ball.''

From 1954 to 1967, he also hosted ``The Bob Chase Show'' Monday through Friday afternoons. During his time, he has interviewed such people as Elvis Presley, the Beatles, Jim Brown, Bob Hope, then-Vice President Richard Nixon, Gordie Howe and Arnold Palmer. His 1957 interview with Elvis is in the Rock and Roll Hall of Fame in Cleveland.

As if he wasn't busy enough, Chase also broadcast approximately 15 NHL games, sometimes filling in for the St. Louis Blues on KMOX and almost left Fort Wayne to join the Blues full time. The problem was the Blues needed him on a weekend when Chase had already committed to covering the Indiana high school basketball tournament.

That opened the door for the Blues to hire someone else, and maybe cost Chase a shot at the Hockey Hall of Fame. The Blues hired future hall-of-famer Dan Kelly instead. Because Chase is not a member of the National Hockey League Broadcasters Association, he's ineligible for the hall of fame.

Another time he turned down a chance to broadcast Detroit Red Wings games.

``If there had ever been an aspiration of mine, it would have been to do the Red Wings games, but they were going to fire Bruce Martyn,'' Chase said. ``When I found that out I told them I wouldn't go. Bruce was a friend of mine from the Upper Peninsula.''

He also turned down chances to go to Washington, Minnesota and Boston, along with several offers from World Hockey Association teams in the early 1970s.

``The only one I took seriously was the St. Louis job. Had that broken right I would have taken it. I went down there on two different occasions, but it worked out the way it was supposed to.''

It turned out that Blues coach Scotty Bowman was friends with Kelly and convinced the team to go in that direction.

``I have no regrets," Chase said. ``I've had more fun as a minor leaguer than I ever would as a major leaguer. In fact, some of my friends who made it and left said it was the loneliest place in the world because there was nobody to talk to, they traveled by themselves, they had no relationship with the players to speak of, and it was quite a culture shock because it wasn't what they thought it was. The money was great, but it just didn't get it done."

It's unimaginable today that Chase would not be doing the Komets games or talking sports on WOWO every morning. There were also several opportunities to leave WOWO and broadcasting to do other, more lucrative jobs, but Chase always stuck with his passion for hockey. Sometimes his work was awe-inspiring.

When the Detroit Vipers joined the IHL during the mid-1990s, they played at the monstrous Palace of Auburn Hills where the press box seemed like a moon shot higher than the Memorial Coliseum press box at the time. It was easily the highest press box in the league, and it didn't help matters that the Vipers wore light blue numerals on their white home jerseys. Because the numbers were not outlined, they were impossible to distinguish from the press box.

Chase didn't know this until the Komets played their first game at Detroit in the Vipers' inaugural season in 1994. While other media members were complaining and frustrated about trying to distinguish players, Chase calmly went about his broadcast and was identifying all the Vipers as if he knew them as well as the Komets.

``I kind of did," he said at the time. ``I just memorized the lines and then picked them out based on their physical characteristics and mannerisms."

The other reporters thought Chase had to be pulling their legs — until the Vipers started scoring goals and Chase never had to make a correction when the official statistics were announced. Somehow he called a perfect game.

Chase's quality also served as inspiration for the next generation of hockey broadcasters, including Mike Emrick who grew up in Lafontaine, Indiana, listening to Chase and then talking with him frequently as a Manchester College student. Emrick often sat in a Memorial Coliseum corner practicing his call of games, and later worked his way to becoming the current dean of NHL broadcasters. As a way to say thank you to Chase, Emrick was the master of ceremonies in 2003 when the Komets celebrated Chase's 50th season behind the Fort Wayne microphone by inducting him into the franchise's hall of fame.

Long-time Kansas City Blades and Grand Rapids Griffins announcer Bob Kaser grew up in Jacksonville, Florida, not exactly a hockey hotbed.

``I was just eight years old and had never been exposed to a sport that is now a huge part of my life," Kaser said in July, 2000. ``One night when I was lying in bed, scanning the radio dial for something good to listen to, I happened on WOWO, and was immediately drawn to it as I listened to Bob describing a game between the Komets and Dayton Gems."

Within a few weeks, Kaser convinced his father to take him to a Jacksonville Rockets pro hockey game. He became so enamored with the sport he soon had nearly all the neighborhood kids playing street hockey, certainly an odd sight in Florida. Kaser became a broadcaster, and in 1994 and 1998 received the Bob Chase Award as the IHL's Broadcaster of the Year. He said it was the greatest award he has received.

``My mission has been, and will always be, to influence as many people as I can in the same way Bob has," Kaser said.

Always humble, Chase said, ``I guess I feel fortunate to feel that people who do that... I feel flattered that I've had that kind of impact on people. I just appreciate I've had an instrument like WOWO at 50,000 watts to have the forum to be there."

He has that kind of effect on everyone. When Indiana's governor awarded Chase a Sagamore of the Wabash in 2003 to celebrate his 50th season with the Komets, as a sign of respect, the players came out of the dressing room during the intermission to sit on the bench and cheer the presentation along with everyone else.

``I never consciously tried to point myself to impact or impress people," he said. ``My dad always told me, 'Be yourself, and if you can't, then get the hell out of the business.' I feel flattered that I've had that kind of impact on people."

The players all have funny stories about Chase, who was always hanging around the team, and even suited up for the Komets in 1956 against the U.S. Olympic team for an exhibition game. Chase got an assist while playing defense.

George Drysdale: "I used to help Bob out on the broadcasts. This was the St. Paul game that went until 1:30 (a.m.) or so (in 1960). Bob and I used to have a few beers up there in a brief case. Well, we ran out and we had been talking for four or five hours. I went down to get something, and I got a bottle of 7-Up. I was walking back up to the radio booth and a guy stopped me. He said take a horn out of that. I did and he filled it up with booze. So we're sitting there and Bob hasn't taken a drink of it yet, and then red light goes on and naturally, that's the time we're going back on the air. Just before the light went off, Bob takes a great big drink out of this thing. He lost his voice for about 15 seconds. I started to laugh. Oh, dear, that was funny."

Len Thornson: "One time we went to Des Moines, and Ken (Ullyot) couldn't come for some reason (separated shoulder). Bob was going to be the coach, too. He was right there giving us advice on the lines and everything. Bob was the most rah-rah guy you ever saw. I think we won both games, and he was the assistant coach from the press box."

Reggie Primeau: "This one trip we were going to Des Moines, and I brought this mouth organ. I was learning to play Christmas carols, and I could play 'Silent Night,' just a few bars. The guys would holler at me to shut up so they could sleep. We get to Des Moines and Bob says, 'Here, give me that.' The guys were in the dressing room, and I was pretending to play it, and they thought I was doing it, but Bob was great. He got a big kick out of that."

Lionel Repka: "I'm in awe how many lives Bob has touched. A lot of people would come up to me in Florida and tell me how they enjoyed the games, and then I'd get fan mail from all over. I got a letter once from a truck driver from Pittsburgh named Repka. He traveled all over and listened to WOWO."

Norm Waslawski: "One time in Des Moines we were in the playoffs and getting ready to get on a plane. Chase puts his hands up to his mouth like a loud speaker and he acted (like) he was paging Reggie (Primeau) to come to a different gate for an urgent message. You could hear it right through the whole terminal. Reggie went and everybody was hiding round the corner. He was a prankster, always pulling stuff."

Gerry Randall: "There are superstars and then there are superstars. The Gordie Howes and the Bob Chases, the longevity-type guys, they are the real superstars. They hung in there and they've been loyal."

Robbie Laird: "I think Bob Chase broadcasting Komets games for 50 years is by far the most significant feat in Komet history, and nothing comes close in my opinion. No amount of goals or championships won comes close to Bob's achievement. Chaser has touched so many people in a positive way."

Muskegon broadcaster Terry Ficorelli: "A few years ago the UHL All-Star Game was in Muskegon (2000), and up to that point I had not had the pleasure of working with Bob. ... What I was impressed with was even though it was an all-star game and Bob has been around seemingly forever, was how excited and enthusiastic he was. He was oozing gusto. After a while it just becomes a job, and you could see with Bob even after all of these years of doing it as we got closer to air time how he was just lighting up. It excited everyone. We had a crew from ESPN, and even they were remarking about how the old guy is still full of enthusiasm and vinegar."

There have been plenty of emotional moments in Chase's life and career. Perhaps the most intense came in 1967. His oldest son Mike had been shot in Viet Nam and was recovering in a hospital when Chase was asked to be the Memorial Day speaker at the Allen County War Memorial Coliseum.

``I really didn't think about it that much," he said. ``Doug Pickell had been a friend of Mike's, and all he can do is talk about Mike. It got to me emotionally. I turn to Jay (Gould) and say, 'You do it, I can't.'

He says, `Like Hell you can't,' and gets up and introduces me. I has shaking so bad I had to stop several times."

Bob Jones, WOWO's public service manager, recorded the speech and Chase was awarded a gold medal by The Freedom Foundation for it.

Things like that make Chase seem larger than life and legendary, but he has never acted that way. During his time with the Komets, Chase has out-lasted five ownership changes, 26 coaches and more than 1,000 players. The Komets have seen two different leagues, including the IHL twice, and nearly 100 opponents come and go.

``Bob amazes me," partner Robbie Irons said. ``If any player I ever played with over the years had the same enthusiasm for every game like he does, they'd be in the NHL. I look up to that. I hope I'm 80 and kick around like he does. How his voice stays that way I have no idea.

``I remember him telling me during one of my first years with the team, he felt that the radio broadcast was like the third arm of the team. There was the game, the players and then the promotion and advertising. He actually believes the radio broadcasting is one part of the success of the team. He feels like he's that much a part of the team, and I'd have to say he definitely is."

Chase has rarely missed calling a game, though sometimes there were conflicts on WOWO with Indiana University basketball. Before the Komets left the International Hockey League in 1999, Chase had broadcast every all-star game the league had played.

When he missed a game on April 2, 1992 because of food poisoning, it was the first time illness had knocked him off a broadcast since 1958 when he had pneumonia. Until he suffered heart problems in 1998, Chase had broadcast all 351 playoff games the Komets had ever played, including four Turner Cup championships and 11 trips to the finals. He missed the final 10 games of that regular season and four playoff games, but came back the next season after quadruple bypass surgery to call 70 games.

``I never set out to do all these crazy things," he said. ``I was just trying to have fun at work."

Despite all of that, he's still just as excited as he was 50 years ago about the game. The reason he continues to broadcast is that he's simply having too much fun to quit. Most people retire to do something they love, but Chase is already doing it.

He can't imagine stopping.

``I'll retire when it ceases to be fun or I lose my faculties to do the games, and the first person who will tell me is my partner, Murph," Chase said. ``It's just too much fun. I enjoy the relationship with the young people, and it keeps me young. As long as this goes and is fun, and the Frankes are happy, I don't see any reason not to keep going."

And he's still going strong as illustrated by another true story: A longtime hockey fan used to listen to Chase broadcast during the 1960s. As his life changed and WOWO's signal changed, the man lost contact with Chase and the Komets. A few years ago he was driving cross country when he picked up a game again, and heard the announcer say he was Bob Chase.

``Boy," the man thought, ``this guy sounds exactly like his dad."

A few years later the man got to meet Chase and see what he looks like. Now he knows it's still the same Bob Chase, just the same as he's always been.

As beloved as Chase is in hockey, he's even more loved in Fort Wayne where he might be the most recognizable person in the city. He may not have grown up in Fort Wayne, but he has certainly become a part of it and was never bothered by his fame.

``It's a real privilege to have it," he said. ``I have trouble… I love it. I'm honored to be accepted. I'm a native now. You earn it, and you just hope you can keep it. I'm honored and thankful."

Bob Chase Awards

1985 Inducted into Avilla Raceway Hall of Fame

1993 Komets retire No. 40 in honor of his 40th season

1993 IHL names Broadcaster of the Year Award the Bob Chase Award

2000 Inducted into Indiana Broadcasters Association Pioneers Hall of Fame Award

2001 Awarded Sagamaore of the Wabash by Indiana Governor Frank O'Bannon

2002 Inducted into Baer Field Speedway Hall of Fame

2003 Named distinguished Hoosier by Governor Frank O'Bannon

2003 Chase added to Komets Hall of Fame in honor of his 50th season

2004 Inducted into Indiana Sportswriters and Sports Broadcasters Hall of Fame

2005 Inducted into intotheboards.net Minor Pro Hockey Hall of Fame

2006 Inducted into Indiana High School Hockey Hall of Fame

Top 10 sports moments

* Covering Big Ten football from 1958 to 1966

* Parnelli Jones introducing turbine engine at Indianapolis 500 in 1967

* Milan-Muncie Central game in 1954

* Komets win 1993 Turner Cup by beating San Diego

* Komets and St. Paul play four overtimes in 1960

* Komets win 1963 Turner Cup by beating Minneapolis

* John Anderson game against Peoria in 1991 Turner Cup Finals

* Broadcasting first NHL game, St. Louis vs. Chicago, in 1968

* Komets win 1973 Turner Cup against Port Huron

* Michigan State-Notre Dame football game from 1966

Top 10 radio moments

* Induction into hall of fames for Indiana Broadcast Pioneers, Indiana Sports Broadcasters and Sagamore of the Wabash honor

* Reopening of renovated Memorial Coliseum in 2002

* Interviewing Vice President Dan Quayle

* Covering President Kennedy's assassination

* Interviewing Elvis Presley in March 1957

* Interviewing Bob Hope

* Interviewing Nat King Cole and Frank Sinatra for Tommy Dorsey tribute

* Interviewing Wayne Gretzky

* Covering Arnold Palmer's first professional win at 1954 Fort Wayne Open

* Watching progress of protégé Mike Emrick

BUD GALLMEIER

CHAPTER 3

Every once in a while, a fed-up Komet player would try to come up with the ultimate slam for Bud Gallmeier.

``I may be a minor league hockey player," the Komet would say, ``but at least I'm on my way up, and I'm not stuck forever in this rinky-dink town."

The slam might have been effective against Gallmeier except he had had turned down several offers from larger papers, including the Chicago Tribune, to stay in the town he loved. Fort Wayne was where he grew up, got married, and raised his family, making his career and his home here. It's impossible to imagine Fort Wayne, or the Komets, without Bud Gallmeier. In many ways, he was better than Fort Wayne, but made it better by staying.

In writing about Paul W. Gallmeier's retirement in 1990, then-News-Sentinel columnist Steve Warden came up with the classic line, ``I never asked, and he never told me what the 'W' stood for. I just assumed it was short for Writer. If it wasn't, then it should have been."

Paul William Gallmeier was born April 5, 1925 in Lutheran Hospital. He had one sibling, an older brother named Chuck who had a short but profound influence on Gallmeier's life in that he was the ultimate big brother to try living up to.

Bud Gallmeier attended St. Paul's Lutheran School and then went to Concordia Lutheran High School, where he graduated in 1943. His claim to fame in high school was that he scored the first seven points for Concordia in the Cadets' first-ever sectional basketball game. He would tell the story every March in The News-Sentinel sports department, so much so that everyone listening could have beaten him to the punch line – if they dared. Warden was the only one who ever did. Of course, Gallmeier never mentioned that Leo beat Concordia 62-31 on February 26, 1943.

During the Depression, Gallmeier's father worked for Packard Piano salesman, and for some reason did quite well during that time running the business. There were troubles though. Gallmeier told of losing a tire once on his car during a time when there were restrictions on rubber. After stopping the car and starting to walk back to get the tire, Gallmeier saw a truck pull up and someone jumped out of the back to grab the tire. They drove away before he could get there.

It was around that time that Gallmeier worked as an usher at Zollner Pistons games at North Side High School during his junior and senior years. Basketball was his first love.

When Gallmeier was attending Concordia, he met second love and eventual wife Trude who went to Central High School and worked as a soda jerk. After they were introduced by friends, he was immediately smitten. While his family had a little money, her family had virtually nothing. Her father had left one day to get a pack of cigarettes and never returned.

After graduation, Gallmeier went to work at the Zollner factory for a short time so he would have a job waiting when he got back from fighting in World War II as a Navy bomber tailgunner. In 1984 he wrote a column about the 1945 Cubs-Tigers World Series that he and his crewmates listened to as they were flying over China.

``I had not been discharged yet when the 1945 World Series was being played. I was still a working member of Navy squadron VPB 119, which since the end of the war had been transformed from a bombing squadron into a weather squadron.

``The squadron was based on Clark Field on the island of Luzon in the Philippines. And by weather squadron it meant whether or not you survived. Our mission was to plot the course of typhoons. It wasn't done by radar. We would fly into the eye of the typhoon and plot its course. And, of course, we then had to fly back out. A Bobby Knight press conference is a gentle breeze by comparison."

While waiting for his official discharge, Gallmeier took a journalism course at a Maryland college and loved it. In those days, a degree was not a necessity to become a newspaper reporter, and he had always liked to write and seemed to have a knack for it. When he was finally discharged, he came home to marry Trude and they moved in with his parents for several years.

Gallmeier's brother Chuck, who was seven years older, was a war hero and won the Navy's Distinguished Flying Cross. After the war, he was continuing to work in Europe as a test pilot when his plane crashed into a gasoline truck that had been parked in the wrong place during an experimental run. The cockpit was blacked out so Gallmeier was flying by using only his instrument board and never saw the truck. He is buried in Arlington National Cemetery.

According to Bud Gallmeier's son Chuck, ``The story goes my father was home with my mother and the doorbell rang and my mother went the door and it was the Air Force there with the bad news. Dad's story and my mom's story was my grandmother said I'm going to bed and she never got out of it. I asked my mother and father for years what exactly she had and the story I was always told was that nobody knew."

Then 21 year-old Bud Gallmeier went to work for the Journal Gazette on March 18, 1947 as a sports department clerk making $40 a week while working from 6 p.m. to 2 a.m. As the third man on a three-man staff, he had covered a few high school games as a stringer but lacked a formal education or much training in the craft.

``He always told me if he had gone to school further, he thought he'd always flunk English comp because he just did it naturally," Gallmeier's son Tim said. ``If he had gone to school and tried to do all the forms or whatever, he figured he'd have been scraping by. Writing was something born in him."

But he wasn't able to make things look so easy at the start of his career. He learned the ropes from Bob Reed and Carl Wiegman who would both later become friendly rivals on the Komets' beat.

In his 1990 retirement column, Gallmeier wrote, ``In 1947, the summer sports schedule evolved around the Zollner Pistons fast-ball team, the

Fort Wayne Daisies of the All-American Girls Baseball League and the GE Club baseball team. On the night in question, all three teams were on the road, and I took the phone calls reporting each of the games.

``The calls came in one after the other and right on deadline... I was feeling pretty good about my work, but not for long. (Managing Editor Park Williams) came storming upstairs and threw the copy down on my desk and barked, 'Here, read this.'

``I did. And shuddered. In the story on the Daisies, I had Hughie Johnson playing first base instead of Vivian Kellogg. In the GE Club story, I had Hughie on first instead of Olin Smith. I don't remember who I had on first for the Pistons.

``Park should have fired me. But he didn't, for which I was eternally grateful. He never brought it up again, but I never forgot it."

Gallmeier worked five years for the Journal Gazette, mostly taking box scores off the phone and writing short stories. Among the few trips he got to take away from the office, he covered the Monroeville Cubs winning the 1948 boys basketball sectional, becoming the first county team to take the title.

The only problem was, Gallmeier was now working nights mostly, and he and Trude had three boys at home. Trude was also taking care of his father and his mother who continued to be bedridden. He would work all night, sleep all morning and then get up to head back to the office. Trude also had never learned to drive. He took her out and tried to teach her once but didn't have the necessary patience, and she swore she'd never go out with him again.

In 1952 he moved to The News-Sentinel so he could work more in the daytime and be home more often with his family in the evenings. The move also allowed him to write more, including covering college beats. He was hired by long-time News-Sentinel sports editor Ben Tenny, whom Gallmeier had first met in 1947 at a Christmas party, though he was always a loyal reader.

``During a conversation with Ben Tenny, sports editor of The News-Sentinel, I spilled a drink on him," Gallmeier recalled in 1988.

``Apparently, Ben didn't hold a grudge, because he hired me five years later."

Hockey became part of Gallmeier's coverage in 1955 – and also a part of his life. He had grown up playing basketball and knew next to nothing about the sport on the ice. He credited new coach Doug ``Crash" McCaig with helping him survive until he thought he knew what he was doing. McCaig lasted only two years with the Komets, but Gallmeier lasted 35.

``I was supposed to be impartial in my pursuit of a story or simple game coverage," he wrote in 1990. ``Sportswriters shouldn't play favorites. But they're also human. I even made a few mistakes in my time. And I was guilty of having more than a few favorites – players as well as teams – during my 35 seasons on the hockey beat."

When Ken Ullyot arrived in 1958, the Komets started to thrive and so did Gallmeier. In the early days, Ullyot was the only person quoted in the stories about the Komets, but the detail of his stories made it obvious Gallmeier had spent a great deal of time talking to the players as well. He had a way of presenting the players' thoughts without actually quoting them.

Gallmeier wrote with compassion and accuracy. He rarely ripped the team, and if he did, they knew they deserved it.

``If he did get after you, you knew there was something happening," all-time Komets leading scorer Len Thornson said. ``It would be the whole team in general."

But there was still a little bit of a fan in Gallmeier. His mood was markedly better if the team was on a winning streak, and if the Komets were on a losing streak, few of his co-workers dared to ask Gallmeier what was wrong with the team. He always had the passion to see the games and to write about them.

``He was with the Komets in the good times and the bad times, and he never complained," Ullyot said. ``I think Bud's forte was just being a regular guy and a good friend. If he was critical in his writings, people just didn't get angry at him. They understood what he was saying. He was a very talented man."

Once after a particularly horrible game, Gallmeier wrote, ``It's likely the Komets have had poorer efforts over their history than they had last night, but I doubt it."

Surprised by Gallmeier's tone, one of his colleagues criticized the lead, saying he had to remain impartial in his reporting, Gallmeier said, ``I did. You didn't see the game. I actually went easy on them."

As Eddie Long said, ``Even though he didn't play every game, he played every game by writing every game."

Gallmeier never went out of his way to criticize the team, but he also only praised players when they deserved it. The players usually appreciated his honesty, and they knew they couldn't put one over on him. If they were playing poorly or giving a weak effort, they knew they couldn't snow Gallmeier because he would never try to fool his readers.

``The thing that was always nice about Bud is that he was always fair to you, win or lose," goaltender Robbie Irons said. ``He knew when you had a bad game, but he didn't always build his stories around the negative. He built around the positive. He was very fair and good to all the players that I've heard of."

Of course Gallmeier had his favorites, but he had a special relationship with Robbie Laird as both a player and a coach.

``Bud was like family to me," Laird said. ``In fact, I used to call him Uncle Bud. I always had a good relationship with all the writers in Fort Wayne, but Bud was extra special. Like after a game where maybe we stunk. He would ask me a question that maybe I thought was too blunt; we might have raised our voices a couple of times to one another, but we were sharing lunch the next day."

After raising their voices, they were usually raising their glasses soon after. Gallmeier was the prototypical stereotype of a sportswriter from his era, the hard-drinking, chain-smoking, poorly dressed man who would hunt and peck at his typewriter to find the magic. He was one of the boys and hung out with the players or even hosted parties in his home for them, something that would be unthinkable today at any level of sports.

``He fell in love with it and he would talk about hockey as if it was a pure sport," Chuck Gallmeier said. ``These guys were over at our house all the time. We would go to school and we would be stars with our buddies because we'd have Len Thornson and Eddie Long coming up to our bedroom at night to say hello to us. Choo Choo (Lionel Repka) and all these folks… Dad just became part of it in the sense that they were friends as much as athletes that he covered.

``That drove my mother crazy because it became so much a part of his life. Mom finally figured out she couldn't win so she embraced it and she used to hang out with these folks, too. They used to have these parties in the garage. And the players were always invited."

After that, the players were always around the Gallmeier household.

``I just remember the laughter and the fun all the time," Gallmeier's daughter Becky Sommer said. ``I was smitten with all of them, and my favorite was Terry Pembroke. I remember the good times they would have at our house, and they were just so friendly, so cool."

The players may be the only people who could keep up with Gallmeier's drinking ability. He used to tell everyone he always got his best stories when he interviewed subjects in bars where they could relax and open up after a beer or two. It certainly helped that the athletes trusted Gallmeier and knew he would never betray a confidence.

A young clerk once got a call at the office from Gallmeier who was at home, telling the clerk to look for something in the bottom drawer of Gallmeier's desk. There were two fifths of Jack Daniels in the drawer. Knowing the first thing the shocked teenager would see, Gallmeier said over the phone, ``That's not what you're looking for."

According to his children, Gallmeier got pulled over a few times, but the police officers all knew him and took him home. He spent so much time at Henry's his face was once included on a mural painted on the side of the building. If he wasn't there, then he was likely at Jack and Johnny's on Wells Street.

Along with his drinking and smoking, Gallmeier was also old-school in that he disliked technology and didn't trust it. He liked writing his stories on a typewriter and then having them transmitted into the computer system. Gallmeier often fought with his computers as much as he worked on them.

``While I was a student at Indiana University in Bloomington, my dad would visit me when he came down to cover a sporting event," Paul Jr. said. ``I once watched him write three stories in an hour and send it off to the paper. I believe he was using a computer at the time provided by the paper. He preferred his old typewriter to `that contraption' as he referred to it."

Once during training with new video display terminals, Gallmeier asked the instructor how to turn on the machine. After Warden told him to rub up against it, Gallmeier rubbed his hand down the side of the machine and said, ``You're so beautiful." That was the end of the class for that day.

After Ben Tenny retired in 1972, Gallmeier became the sports editor of The News-Sentinel. That meant he had first pick of all the assignments, but he kept Purdue and the Komets while sometimes sliding in a few plum jobs such as heavyweight title fights.

``Out of all the siblings, I was probably the most fortunate because I got to go with him on all the trips, like the 1976 World Series," Tim Gallmeier said. ``My dad and Bob Ford from the Muncie paper, I never saw two guys like that who could put the beer away and get up the next morning and still be functional. I was green to the gills and ready to die and they were already having Bloody Marys. `Guys don't you ever get drunk? They just laughed and laughed. I'm green to the gills and they looked great."

Gallmeier often took his children on road trips. Becky liked going to the hockey games and the Indianapolis 500.

``When I was confirmed in grade school, that Sunday the Komets were playing for the Turner Cup against Port Huron (in 1973) and I remember Dave Welker coming to the house and saying they had a bus ready to go," Becky said. ``Dad was asking me, do you mind if I go, but I said only if you take me with you. That was the first championship game I ever saw. Everybody kind of understood, and my brother Tim and my brother Kevin had gone on another bus. I remember we had the greatest time and saw them win it. I wouldn't have missed that for the world. It was just so cool."

Late in his career, Gallmeier liked taking Becky's daughter Katie to games in Kalamazoo. For some reason Trude never wanted to go on the road trips, though Bud continually offered.

Besides including his children on road trips, Gallmeier often mentioned them in his columns. Paul Jr., then 19, was serving in Viet Nam on December 24, 1968 when his father wrote a column addressed to him: ``But there has been a change in our Christmas the past two years – a change which thousands of other families also have experienced, some for longer than two years. We haven't been a complete family because you have been away. And because of this, Christmas doesn't seem the same.

``The message of Christmas is Peace on Earth, Good Will to Men. But the message hasn't been getting through. There has been unrest over most of the world. Few nights are silent in the Holy Land. Shepherds still quake but for different reasons."

Understandably, it is still Paul Jr.'s favorite all-time column by his father.

To say that Gallmeier covered the Fort Wayne sports scene would be somewhat inaccurate and inadequate. He was Fort Wayne's sports historian, painting pictures of the actions with his typewriter, adding his unique writing and humor to the mix. He captured the people and the emotions of events.

``He always told me that what he did for a living allowed him to get to places where these people couldn't be, and he always felt that was special," Chuck said. ``He could open doors for people."

In perhaps his best-remembered start to a story, on May 29, 1990 he wrote of the Indianapolis 500, ``Arie Luyendyk wasn't happy with the way his car handled in traffic, so he drove away from it and won the greatest race in the world.''

Another column included this story about meeting former NHL Commissioner Clarence Campbell at his hotel room to pick up a ticket: ``I met Campbell, who died Sunday at the age of 78, just once, 18 years ago. I can still see Campbell as he opened the door of his room at the Sheraton Cadillac Hotel in Detroit. It wasn't the picture I expected. He didn't look very distinguished. But, then, nobody does wearing only long underwear.''

As easy as Gallmeier's writing was read as he made it seem effortless, he agonized over it.

``My father was a little bit insecure,'' Tim said. ``He was always concerned his readers wouldn't like him or like what he wrote. He always had us read his stories before he sent them in, but he always wanted to be reinforced. We relished that.''

Each night after the dinner table had been cleared, Gallmeier would sit down to write his column. A couple hours later he'd ask Trude or one of the children to read it before he sent it in. If everyone had already gone to bed, he'd wake one of them.

``I always felt like it was not for me to say if something was wrong, he just needed confirmation,'' Chuck said. ``The key thing was you never said anything critical.''

Maybe the most astonishing thing about Gallmeier was his remarkable recall. Gallmeier was gifted with an incredible memory that allowed him to interview subjects without using a tape recorder and rarely taking a note.

``It was always a puzzle to me and we don't know how he did it,'' Chuck said. ``Everybody was shocked by it that he never took notes, and often it wasn't a hockey player or a coach or a basketball player. He never used a tape recorder. Maybe as he got older he might have used one a little.''

About the only time anyone remembers him using one was during an interview with Muhammad Ali which has become a family heirloom.

Some of the stories are almost mythical. When Gregg Pilling was hired to coach the Komets in the summer of 1977, Bob Chase sent Gallmeier to Pilling's hotel room the night before a morning press conference. Gallmeier had been partying, and by the time he arrived, looked like he could barely stand. After guiding Gallmeier to the couch, Pilling offered him another beer. As Gallmeier wavered back and forth sitting on the couch, the interview started. An hour later, after seeing Gallmeier to the door, an irate Pilling called to wake Chase and complain. Chase laughed, making Pilling even madder, but told the coach to relax and everything would be fine.

The next day Pilling picked up the paper, read the story and realized there were no mistakes, no misquotes and no problems. He called Chase to apologize.

``I asked him 100 times in my lifetime, `Dad, how do you do that?' '' Chuck said. ``I don't think it was photographic. It was just something... I don't know how he did it, but I can't think of a single time that he ever had a coach or a ballplayer call him and say he misquoted him. And it wasn't sports-agese, either. It was what they said.''

Occasionally while being interviewed, players said, they would look over at Gallmeier's notepad and see chicken scratches. When the paper came out the next day, they always wondered how he could be so accurate.

``He was very proud of the fact that he never used his tape recorder,'' Laird said. ``He never misquoted me.''

Because of Fort Wayne Newspapers' rules at the time, News-Sentinel writers were not allowed into the building until 6 a.m. That meant Gallmeier was often working on short sleep and was hung over when he wrote.

``During an interview, he had the uncanny ability to enjoy a bottle or two of beer without taking notes and write a column the next day and quote you verbatim,'' Lionel Repka said. ``I thought there was no way in hell he could write anything, and boom, the next day he never missed a lick. His memory bank was like a steel trap."

That memory also meant his children could never pull a fast one. There was never any fudging by saying they thought he said a later time for a curfew.

``You couldn't beat him," Tim said. ``If you thought something was going on back in the past and if you thought you were right, it turned out you were wrong because he had that wonderful memory. You never had a chance."

Even later in his life, Gallmeier could remember specific incidents and recall them with almost perfect clarity. If he was off on a date, it was only by a day or two.

Some of that hard living caught up with Gallmeier in 1983. Instead of finishing a Komets' game, he came home and said he felt sweaty and clammy. Trude did not drive, so she quickly called a neighbor, Pam Bangert who was a nurse, and she drove them to the hospital.

``My dad said, `If I didn't have a heart attack then, I was having one in the car,' because I guess she drove like crazy," Becky said.

He needed a quadruple bypass.

``I won't say it was a snap," he wrote in a Christmas Eve column that year. ``Anybody who tells you it is hasn't gone through it. And I'm not ashamed when I say I was scared. More so than that day long ago when I saw flak for the first time outside the window of my tail turret."

During the column, he thanked Indiana University for producing fine doctors as well as basketball players which had to hurt because of his regard for Purdue. He also talked about how Christmas was more special that year and how he suddenly had more patience with everything.

That doesn't mean he stuck to his diet.

``He loved the Rubens and I busted him a couple of times at Jack and Johnny's," Chuck said. `` `Just don't tell your mother,' and I'd say `OK, Dad.' "

When Gallmeier returned to his typewriter, he was as feisty as ever, including a confrontation with Bobby Knight at the Mad Anthonys golf tournament in 1987. It was shortly after John Feinstein's book ``A Season on the Brink" was released, and Knight quit attending press conferences after games. Instead he would send an assistant coach or a public relations guy to fill in, or the reporters would be handed a typewritten sheet with comments supposedly from Knight.

``So Dad decided to not use Bob's name in his stories," Chuck said. ``He'd call him the coach at Indiana or Indiana's coach. At the Mad Anthonys, Knight brought it up. 'You son of a bitch, what kind of f----- BS is that?' And Dad says, 'Bobby, once you come out and start talking to the reporters, I'll be more than happy to use your name again, but not until.' "

Neither man was shy about using profanity. Knight supposedly said something smart back to Gallmeier who supposedly responded with a slam referring to an incident in Knight's past. Then Knight allegedly grabbed Gallmeier and threw him into the lockers.

``Some people said he should sue him, but Dad always said, 'He respects me now.' From that point on he never had trouble with Knight again. I remember when Dad died, we got a call from Keady and we got a letter from Knight. I know that's the only thing that gets Knight to respect you is when you stand up to him."

Gallmeier did slow down his work load and spent more time at home as the 1980s wound down. He walked constantly after his heart surgery, and used to worry about Mike Ditka because he was always chewing gum, wondering if it was sugar-free.

He covered the Komets full-time through the 1989-90 season, the last of the years under David Welker's ownership. Just before he retired, the Komets added his name with no number to their retired numbers banner to honor his 35 years covering the team.

``I think it was one of the most emotional moments of his life, and my father was not a hugger, but it was tough to get past that," Chuck said. ``I remember calling and it was one of the first times I could hear in his voice that he was choking up."

``My dad never thought he was all that spectacular or anything special," Becky said. ``When they were oohing and aahing all over him, he just wasn't real comfortable."

It was certainly an emotional moment for everyone else.

``He's in the classification of Bob Chase as far as building hockey in Fort Wayne," Eddie Long said.

``He wasn't known as a writer, but as part of the team," Robbie Irons said. ``He had the title of writer, but he was always there, for practices, road trips. He was personally involved and you knew that when he was asking the questions. It wasn't just a job for him."

Gallmeier retired May 30, 1990, though he still continued to cover the Komets and fill in on a part-time basis. Each Monday he would call the office, ``Don't you have something else you need to be covering this week?" No, not really, Bud. ``Well, get something because I'm bored." He could barely tolerate watching a game from the stands, saying he always felt like he should be taking notes or doing something, anything.

It was too bad because that was the summer the Franke brothers bought the Komets and they got hot. Suddenly, everyone in Fort Wayne was a Komets fan again. Gallmeier helped out by writing the team's 40th anniversary yearbook. He also spent time easing the transition of those who tried to fill in for him – even though those he helped knew he could never be replaced.

But most of the time he spent playing with his grandchildren in the backyard pool.

Truthfully, Gallmeier never wanted to retire.

``He was always disappointed that he didn't write a book," Chuck said. ``I think he just ran out of energy. He was tired. He was not well, and I think he knew that."

The bypass lasted him nine years before the heart he shared with so may finally stopped beating on September 11, 1992 at Parkview Memorial Hospital from congestive heart failure. Bud Gallmeier was 67.

He was survived by Trude, sons Bud Jr., Chuck, Kevin, Tim and daughter Becky and six grandchildren.

Along with Chuck, Becky delivered part of the eulogy.

``I wasn't sure what to say but I brought up the fact that the proudest day of his life was walking down the aisle at our church when I got married," she said. ``We got married on the day that was the Old Oaken Bucket game. We just chose the date, and I remember him telling me, 'You remember what date that is, don't you?' My dad told me he wouldn't have traded that for the world, and that was the happiest moment of his life, walking me down the aisle and the party we had. He stayed for everything, and they had an open bar. The last picture we have of him is he has his pockets turned out because he didn't have any money left."

Gallmeier was buried at Greenlawn Cemetery.

``We drove past The News-Sentinel and saw the flag at half staff," Becky said. ``My children were in awe of that because my dad was just a common man."

But anyone who ever read him or met him knew he was anything but common.

In his retirement column, Gallmeier wrote, ``Not many people get paid for doing what they love. I'm one. It's been fun. I haven't made a lot of money, but I know I've been the envy of many people who have made a lot more."

Instead, he took everyone along for the ride to the race, the court or the rink through his typewriter.

Bud Gallmeier

Covered the Fort Wayne Komets for 35 seasons

A recreational softball league was named after him in 1993

Worked at the Journal Gazette from 1947 to 1952

Worked at The News-Sentinel from 1952 to 1990

Covered Indiana University's national championships in 1976 and 1981

Covered the Indianapolis 500 for 31 years

Covered Notre Dame's 1973 Sugar Bowl victory over Alabama to win the national title

Covered three Komets' Turner Cup championships

Inducted into the Komets Hall of Fame in 1988

Name added to the Komets' retired banners in 1990

Received Virgil Sweet Award from Indiana Basketball Coaches Association in 1990

Inducted into Avilla Speedway Hall of Fame in 1990

Inducted into Indiana Sportswriters and Sportscasters Hall of Fame in 2002

LEN THORNSON

CHAPTER 4

While Don Graham and Ryan Taylor were researching their book ``50 years of Komets Hockey" in 2001 and 2002, they talked to more than 75 former Komets and asked almost all of them, ``Who is the greatest player you ever played with?"

Every player from the 1950s and 1960s had the same answer, except one, the player everyone else identified.

``We had a lot of great players," Len Thornson said.

Except none were able to match Thornson's statistics or individual accomplishments. He finished his 13-season International Hockey League career in 1969 with a league record 1,382 points. From his first Fort Wayne season in 1958-59 until his next-to-last year in 1967-68, Thornson scored more than 100 points seven times and had three other seasons of 99, 93 and 97 points. During the 99-point season, Thornson reached that total in 52 games before being knocked out for the season with a broken leg.

Seven times he was named the league's most valuable player, and The Hockey News named him the IHL's all-time greatest player in 1997. No one else could even be considered.

``He brought up the level of the league," long-time Komets coach Ken Ullyot said. ``His talent was on display every game because he played hard. The challenge was to opponents to stop him, and they couldn't."

About the only thing that could stop Thornson was the depth of the Montreal Canadiens, who controlled his NHL rights. Despite all his amazing efforts, Thornson never made it to the NHL because Montreal was winning five straight Stanley Cups from 1956 to 1960 and usually had its lineup set before training camp. At just about the same time, the Canadiens' farm club in Cincinnati was winning five straight IHL Turner Cups.

Thornson never really got a chance, even when he proved he deserved one. Before the 1959-60 season, Thornson tried out with the Canadiens' farm club in Cleveland of the American Hockey League. He was 26 years old and coming off his first IHL MVP award, and then he dominated the camp.

``I had the greatest training camp I've ever had in my life," Thornson said. ``I think we played 4 or 5 exhibition games and I got 7 or 8 goals and something like 15 or 16 points. We played all these AHL teams and even the Canadiens."

Instead of taking Thornson with them or leaving him in Cleveland, the Canadiens wanted him to play for another of their farm teams in Montreal which would have meant moving his family and making less money than he would with the Komets. He gave up and called Ullyot to work out a new contract.

As far as Thornson knows, no other NHL team – and this was during the six-team era – contacted Montreal about acquiring his rights. One time the Canadiens lost six games in a row, and Thornson got his hopes up, but the phone never rang.

``The thing that happens in the NHL is by the time you get to 25 or 26 years old, they want the young guy and they aren't interested in you any more," Thornson said.

But why not just one NHL game?

``When one or two spots opened up every year, I was one of 150 guys trying out," Thornson said.

Thornson, and many of his teammates, missed their chance to play in the NHL when expansion came in 1967. By then, they were too old or too well established in Fort Wayne to take a chance.

``These guys were good hockey players," Thornson teammate Eddie Long said. ``I would say that all the guys I played with, if the NHL had as many teams then as they have now, I think all of us would have had a good opportunity. Would they have made it? I don't know."

The way the Canadiens acquired Thornson's rights could never happen today but was common during the 1940s and 1950s. The player draft didn't exist, so teams sent scouts across Canada looking for players and signed anyone with a hint of promise at age 16 – or even earlier in some cases.

Thornson always showed plenty of promise. He was born February 4, 1933 to Thomas and Betty Thornson, the oldest of four boys. His father worked for Coca-Cola for 39 years as a cooper, building barrels, while his mother was a homemaker.

Like every other boy, Thornson learned to skate by age 6 and then joined the neighborhood games. Because this was during World War II, there were no cars so the younger boys played in the streets and back alleys.

``You had to stickhandle like crazy through everybody," Thornson said. ``You always wanted to be the stickhandler."

In the era before television, computers or even radio in some cases, there were usually more than 10 kids playing after school every day. During the summers, they went across to the school yard and played ball hockey.

With that training, there were six friends who grew up and played together on organized teams once they turned 11. They never lost a game in Bantam A, lost only the championship game in Bantam B, and went undefeated in Midget and Juvenile.

Their coach was Dennis Ball who later became an assistant general manager with the New York Rangers. By the time the boys turned 16, they were being scouted by the Canadiens.

``There were always scouts after you all the time," Thornson said. ``The guy who was the scout for the Canadiens was always there and trying to lure you into signing by doing different things. I remember he always had six or seven hockey sticks under his arm, and in those times, they were worth gold."

Four of the boys signed with Montreal and they played together for a total of seven years. Part of the fun was flying to Montreal as soon as their playoffs were done to watch the Canadiens play and practice with them.

Thornson always played center, but he doesn't remember if there was a reason why. With his passing ability and ability to see the ice, he seemed like a natural pivot man. He could turn defensemen around and goaltenders into pretzels with his moves. He wasn't the greatest stickhandler, but no one could get the puck away from him, and he was an exceptional puck carrier, moving it through the neutral zone with ease.

While playing with the Winnipeg Canadiens in junior, the highlight was playing in the Memorial Cup finals in 1953. Winnipeg beat Lethbridge in the West finals but had to wait 24 or 25 days in April for Barrie to arrive because the East playoffs took so much longer to complete. By that time, the boys had lost their edge.

The next year the Canadiens lent Thornson to New Westminster where he was replacing a departed center named Ken Ullyot who had started his coaching career. Thornson was the youngest player on the team.

``In those days younger players sat beside the coach for the first 20 games or so and hardly got on the ice," he said. ``You killed penalties and stuff, and maybe you played a little more on the road. Their idea was you were there to learn."

Thornson scored 10 goals and 20 points in his one season with New Westminster. The following year, Thornson was moved by Montreal to the Quebec Hockey League's Shawinigan Falls which went on to win the Canadian Professional Hockey Championship.

``The first goal I ever got was against (future NHL hall of famer) Glenn Hall," Thornson said. ``I walked in on him and went top drawer, bingo. I still remember that one. Most of the goals I got were important, but that doesn't mean you got on the ice any more. It didn't work that way."

Thornson played in Shawinigan Falls for two seasons, but that wasn't as monumental as what happened away from the rink. Margaret Brown was two years younger than Thornson, but he had noticed her in school. He was too shy to ask her out so a buddy did it for him.

``I remember Cliff Phillips set it up," she said. ``I thought he was asking me out."

``So she said yes," Thornson said nearly 54 years later with a chuckle.

``I thought he was asking me to the movies and I said sure, and he said, 'Well you're going with Len Thornson.' I said 'Who?' I really I didn't know him."

They went together for quite a few months but then broke up. That didn't last.

``One time I was coming home and I was riding the bus," she said. ``It was in the evening and I got off at my corner where I just lived five houses down, but he got off the bus, too, and he lived way down the way. I said, 'Where are you going?' and he said, 'I'm walking you home.' And we started up again. I guess it was meant to be."

She joked that she wasn't sure if he was coming to see her or her father who was a doctor because he always seemed to have a broken finger or nose.

They got engaged while Thornson was playing at New Westminster, though both claim he never actually proposed. They set the date for May 14, 1955, but the problem was he was still in Quebec playing for Shawinigan Falls until May 5.

``I don't think the minister thought I existed," Thornson said.

``Then he took me far from home and far from family, but you know I wouldn't change it for anything," Margaret said.

The Thornson's first child, Mike, was born in Indianapolis on November 23, 1956, someplace his father really never expected to play. The Canadiens wanted to ship him to Chicoutimi, but Thornson wasn't thrilled about that so they offered to send him to the United States instead. Montreal was going to send Thornson to Cincinnati, but the Mohawks were on a 10-game winning streak and he got sent to Indianapolis instead.

While playing in Indianapolis, Thornson played for Leo Lamoureux for whom the IHL later named the trophy which was awarded to the league's leading scorer. Thornson didn't have that kind of success with the Chiefs, though, and he didn't stay there for very long.

Ramon Perry, one of the original owners of the Komets, had started a consortium of Fort Wayne businessmen who put a team in Huntington, West Virginia, to make sure the league had enough teams to function. The Hornets were struggling and made a trade to send George Hayes to Indianapolis for Thornson and Len Ronson. The trade didn't help as Hayes finished with 44 points in 30 games to lead Indianapolis to the Turner Cup Finals. In 56 games that season, Thornson scored 14 goals and 33 points, but it wasn't enough to save the Hornets from folding.

To replace Huntington, the IHL welcomed Louisville to the league for the 1957-58 season, and Thornson and Ronson received a letter telling them to report to Fort Wayne.

``I said, `You know Margaret, something has to happen or we have to pack it in,' '' Thornson said. ``I needed to produce or go home and get a job. Do I want to stay home or do I want to still try to keep something going? I decided to give it one last shot, but I also decided to do things my way a little bit rather than what they wanted.''

Amazingly, things started clicking for Thornson. Playing with Ronson and Billy Richardson on his wings, he scored 34 goals and 81 points to lead the Komets in scoring. The Komets made the playoffs for the third time in their brief six-year history but lost to Indianapolis in the semifinals. Thornson was rewarded with his first all-star team selection, named to the second team behind Marc Boileau of Indianapolis.

Thornson had his answer about his future. Though things were looking up on the ice, there was big trouble off it as the Komets reported losses of $87,000. Ken Ullyot was hired as general manager that summer, and after examining the books, figured he better save money by naming himself coach, too. He brought in his friend Colin Lister to handle the office. Training camp was held in Troy to also save money.

``I rode down with Colin," Thornson said. ``I was the first player he ever met and we're driving to Troy. He thinks I know how to get there, and I think he knows how to get there. We had a pretty good thing going between the two of us because we yapped the whole way down."

Ullyot's training camp was difficult. A product of the New York Rangers' coaching system, he stressed fundamentals and taught them by using sometimes monotonous but effective drills.

``Ken would drive guys crazy because they were the most boring practices imaginable," Thornson said. ``You'd go skating down the ice and you'd have to drop the puck and keep going. Nobody wanted to do that stuff, but it was tremendously good for us when you think about it. He was in his glory."

With Thornson scoring 30 goals and 103 points to earn his first MVP award, the Komets improved by four wins in the regular season and reached their first Turner Cup Finals before losing to Louisville. Ullyot kept Thornson and Ronson together and added Norm Waslawski after Maisonneauve left. With Thornson setting them up, Ronson scored 39 goals and Waslawski 40.

The next season was even better, as Thornson finished with 107 points by helping Ronson score a league-record 71 goals and 109 points of his own. Replacing Waslawski, Bob McCusker scored 34 goals and 89 points. The Komets tore through the IHL with a 50-16-2 record.

``It was like we weren't ever going to lose, and if we did lose, then something was wrong," Thornson said.

But the Komets did lose in the Turner Cup Finals to St. Paul, dropping the key Game 4 in the fourth overtime. Despite out-shooting St. Paul 76-57 and getting 46 shots in the overtimes, the Komets finally lost on a fluke goal. Saints goaltender and former Komet Glenn Ramsay was just too good.

``Rammer beat us," Thornson said. ``There's no way they should have beaten us. We should have beaten them easy. It was just a tremendously good team, and to lose it that way just blew your mind."

Once again Thornson found a good distraction off the ice. Daughter Wendy was born February 18, 1959, and son Brian was born December 31, 1961. Broadcaster Bob Chase joked on the air that Brian's name was ``Tax Credit." Today there are nine grandchildren and two great grandchildren.

The 1960 loss seemed to crush the spirit of the Komets, and it didn't help when Thornson suffered a broken leg 52 games into the 1960-61 schedule. His start of 35 goals and 99 points was remarkable as Ken Yackel of Minneapolis won the IHL scoring title with 114 points – playing 20 more games than Thornson. Linemates Jimmy Baird and Joe Kastelic also had big years.

Thornson came back the next season to win his second scoring title with 122 points. He also started a remarkable string of five straight MVP awards, sharing the 1962-63 honor with teammate Eddie Long.

``He reminded me of Jean Beliveau," Long said. ``Lennie was smooth and really very deceptive. He was faster than people thought he was. He'd do the same move and these guys would go for it every time. Pull the puck back and go. He was an all-around player really. If you played the position with Lennie, he knew where you were. He knew where everybody was on the ice, too. The one thing he didn't do, and he probably would have gotten more goals was shoot the puck. He had a good shot, but he didn't shoot."

Thornson always felt he was a better passer, partly because he could hold the puck long enough to get the puck where he wanted it go – which is where Long often came in.

``We always knew where each other was, and it was kind of a neat thing," Thornson said. ``I think some of the best goal-scoring years he had was when he was playing with me. He was probably as good a goal scorer as I was ever around. He was a true goal scorer. His hustle got him to that place. We had guys like Dubchak and Ronson who might have been more talented goal scorers, but Eddie always found a way to get it done all the time. He was always ready to go."

Sometimes Thornson didn't get off to the best starts, but he always finished strong. One season Ullyot fined him $100 for missing a plane while Thornson was actually sitting on the plane. He was trailing the scoring race by about 25 points at the time but still came back to win the title by 17 points.

Ullyot never doubted Thornson's talent, his commitment or his love of the game. He once said Thornson was the most loyal player he had ever worked with, along with being the most talented.

``He could give you the puck and take it back, and by that time, you had fallen on your face," Ullyot said. ``He was just so gentle with it. He was a treasure to play with. To play with him, you were getting the puck wide open many times."

 Building around the consistency of Thornson and Long, the Komets finally broke through and won their first title in 1963. Thornson was remarkable in the playoffs with 8 goals and 19 points during the 11 postseason games.

It was at about that time the Thornsons decided to make Fort Wayne their permanent home. Mike was ready to start school, and Len kept finding business opportunities in the community. At different times he owned a landscaping company, a carpet and furniture cleaning business and he also got involved with a builder and helped build five homes, hiring some teammates to do some extra painting.

The funny thing is, none of the Komets mainstays of that time came to Fort Wayne with expectations of living there forever, but they built such strong bonds on and off the ice that they eventually couldn't imagine leaving. Because they were so close, it made the transition into the community easier.

``We used to play slo-pitch softball," Thornson said. ``We had Reggie, Waz, Teddy Wright, Chuck, myself. Roger. Every one of our players was left-handed. we were the only team in the league to have a left-handed batter and we had eight of them. Chuck's father-in-law was our pitcher and he was right-handed. Then they talked about us playing fast pitch, and we started playing that for a while. All the guys were together like that all the time."

Using that camaraderie, the Komets almost won three Turner Cups in a row. After beating Minneapolis in 1963, they returned to the finals in 1964 only to lose to Toledo with the help of a controversial call. Merv Dubchak had a key goal called back on a late call for a two-line pass that the Komets still dispute. Fort Wayne lost the next game at Toledo 2-1.

The Komets came back even stronger in 1965 and whipped Des Moines to earn their second cup.

``It all comes back down to you can be playing well, but you still have to play better defensively in the playoffs," Thornson said.

But Thornson also continued his offensive numbers, scoring 115 points in 1962-63, 108 in 1963-64 and 93 in 1964-65. He picked it back up with 105 in 1965-66 and 139 in 1966-67 to set the league record. The line of Thornson, Merv Dubchak and Johnny Goodwin averaged 5.2 points per game that season, the highest average ever by a Komets' line.

The funny thing is, Thornson might have been one of the slowest skaters on the team, and he admits Reggie Primeau was a much better stickhandler than he was.

``He was real smooth with the puck, he just kind of floated," Primeau said. ``One thing he couldn't do is skate backwards, and we used to tease the heck out of him about it."

``He still can't," Lionel Repka said. ``But he was a better skater than he got credit for. Once he got going, he was a little faster than you thought he was because he looked slow, and he never seemed to get caught from behind."

There's a good reason for that, Thornson said.

``That's one of the thing I learned in Montreal from a guy by the name of Dickie Moore," Thornson said. ``He might be one of the better players I ever saw in my life. He was another one who was a slow little sucker but you couldn't catch him. One day he told me, `Going down the ice, you use a long stride the same as I do, but the greatest thing you have going for you is a change of pace. It should always really look like you are going, but you should always have that last little burst left.' It always worked."

Ullyot always swore it was because opponents got caught watching Thornson dangle the puck rather than his feet as he went around them. Thornson was also very deceptive with his stick and his brain. Defensemen never knew what he was going to do. A favorite move was one he learned from Freddy Shero, who later became coach of the Philadelphia Flyers.

``Freddy told me the biggest thing you can do is learn how to trick somebody," Thornson said. ``He said, 'Shoot, and miss the puck.' So you make like you are shooting like crazy and kind of miss the puck so it dribbles along. As soon as you do that the defenseman flinches, and it's all set up for you."

Teammate Teddy Wright used to call Thornson ``Snake" because he always seemed able to slither between defenders. He had great balance and was impossible to clear from the front of the net.

``It wasn't courage with him, it was just natural instinct," Ullyot said. ``He'd be standing in front of that net and they'd try to knock him down and they couldn't. He didn't need coaching so to speak because he had the fundamentals down pat."

It seemed no one could slow Thornson down, but an injury finally stopped him. During the 1968-69 season, Thornson took over from Ullyot as a playing coach. The Komets were on a tear when they went to Port Huron on November 17. Thornson and the Flags' Nelson Tremblay were going for a faceoff when Tremblay raised his stick straight up, catching Thornson in his right eye.

``I knew right away I was done," Thornson said.

He was legally blind in the eye for a period of time, and eventually came back wearing a helmet after trying contacts and glasses. During his first game back, he suffered a broken cheekbone when he was hit by a Terry Pembroke shot. He never saw the puck.

Thornson kept trying, finishing with 50 points in 46 games but he sometimes had trouble seeing an open winger, something that never happened before.

Ullyot took over behind the bench, but the Komets were not a very good team that season. Primeau, Repka, Teddy Wright and Merv Dubchak all suffered severe injuries after Thornson. They were 8-5-1 when Thornson was injured and finished 24-33-15 with only three road wins. Dayton swept Fort Wayne in three games during the first round of the playoffs.

Thornson's eye never recovered (it was eventually fixed during a 2004 surgery), and he was forced to retire at age 36. He finished with 479 goals, 903 assists and 1,382 career points – along with only 101 penalty minutes. He finished among the league's top 10 scorers for a remarkable 11 consecutive seasons. Somewhere along the way, he had passed Long as the IHL's all-time leading scorer, but no one knew it at the time.

``Nothing was ever mentioned or said about it," Thornson said. ``It never existed. The only thing that was ever said was Bob and Bud (Gallmeier) came up to me one time and said they had to do something for me. I'm like, why? And Bud said, `You're coming up on your thousandth point.' I had no idea."

He passed that milestone on January 5, 1966. The Komets gave him a plaque and a bonus as a reward.

Though he had been planning on playing at least a couple more seasons, fate helped Thornson make the adjustment into retirement. On the Friday before he got hurt, Thornson was invited to lunch by a hockey fan who wanted him to meet Jack Hayes, a State Farm agent.

``After I got hurt, Tuesday morning there's Jack Hayes sitting by the front door to offer me a job," Thornson said.

He eventually opened his own branch and became one of the state's top managers before retiring in 1995.

There were a few honors still coming from Thornson's playing career. He was inducted into the Manitoba Hall of Fame in 1993, and in 1997 The Hockey News named him the IHL's all-time best player.

Thornson's IHL scoring record lasted an amazing 32 years before Cleveland center Jock Callander passed him in February of 2000. If Thornson had not gotten hurt, his records might have lasted for all-time as the IHL folded in 2001 before being re-started in 2007. Callander broke the record at age 38 by playing in nearly 300 more games.

``All the more power to him," Thornson said at the time. ``Heck, yeah, you want to keep a record, but I'm surprised it's lasted more than 30 years. There's a lot of players who played here for a long time."

Thornson was hot news again, and his accomplishments were even more impressive looking back through history.

``What's funny is that if I'd gone to the NHL, they'd never be there," Thornson said. ``Coming to Fort Wayne and staying here is the best thing that ever happened to me."

Len Thornson's careers statistics Playing Regular season *Playoffs

Season	Team	League	GP	G	A	PTS	PIM	GP	G	A	PTS	PIM
52-53	Buffalo	AHL	3	0	1	1	0	*	*	*	*	*
53-54	New Westminster	WHL	61	10	12	22	0	7	0	2	2	0
54-55	Shawinigan Falls	QHL	27	9	7	16	0	*	*	*	*	*
55-56	Shawinigan Falls	QHL	47	11	9	20	8	*	*	*	*	*
56-57	Huntn-Indpls	IHL	56	14	19	33	9	*	*	*	*	*
57-58	Fort Wayne	IHL	64	47	81	12	4	2	3	5	0	
58-59	Fort Wayne	IHL	58	30	73	103	0	11	4	16	20	0
59-60	Fort Wayne	IHL	67	36	71	107	6	13	7	7	14	0
60-61	Fort Wayne	IHL	52	35	64	99	6	DNP	*	*	*	*
61-62	Fort Wayne	IHL	67	32	90	122	14	*	*	*	*	*
62-63	Fort Wayne	IHL	70	32	83	115	10	11	8	11	19	4
63-64	Fort Wayne	IHL	67	37	71	108	6	12	5	9	14	0
64-65	Fort Wayne	IHL	67	41	52	93	10	10	12	6	18	0
65-66	Fort Wayne	IHL	66	36	69	105	2	6	1	5	6	2
66-67	Fort Wayne	IHL	71	46	93	139	10	13	87	14	4	*
67-68	Fort Wayne	IHL	68	38	59	97	10	6	3	8	11	0
68-69	Fort Wayne	IHL	46	15	35	59	6	6	3	2	5	2

KEN ULLYOT

CHAPTER 5

It's something of an urban legend in Komets history that Ken Ullyot signed his first and only Fort Wayne contract on the back of a pack of cigarettes. The truth is Ullyot actually signed it on his heart.

After the Komets reported losses $87,000 at the end of the 1957-58 season, the team was close to going out of business after only five seasons. Co-owner Harold Van Orman tried convincing Ken Wilson to leave as Troy's general manager and come to Fort Wayne, but Wilson was worried if he left Troy would fold. He stayed – and Troy ended up being extremely important that season – but said he had the perfect guy to come to Fort Wayne. No truer words were ever spoken about the Komets.

Wilson got on the phone to his childhood friend Ullyot. They had met in Saskatoon in 1936, growing up three blocks apart playing hockey.

After his playing days, Wilson developed a relationship with Eddie Shore who sent him to run Troy. Ullyot started coaching in the New York Rangers organization, working through the Western Hockey League and eventually becoming Fort Wayne's hockey godfather. Without him, it's doubtful the Komets, the International Hockey League and maybe even minor league hockey in the Midwest would have lasted. At times, it all barely survived anyway.

``I knew Van Orman who owned the team, and they were drawing pretty well but they had terrible management," Wilson said. ``He asked me if I knew anybody who could run the team, and I said, `I have just the guy for you.' Harold asked how much money they would have to pay someone like that, and I said $150 a week. He said, `OK, you phone him and tell him he has a job.' Kenny wasn't too excited so I told him to grab a plane and get down here and talk to the guy. He had nothing to lose. We got his flight number and I met him at the airport in Fort Wayne and we went to Van Orman's house."

The negotiations grew to include much more than just coaching the team.

``I came here because Harold Van Orman told me, `You can become a partner with us,' '' Ullyot said. ``I asked how I could trust that, and Harold said, `Because I told you so.' Harold Van Orman and Ray Perry were the most honest people I ever dealt with. They kept their word on everything. I asked them about a contract, and Harold said, `Didn't I shake hands with you? There's a contract, you don't have to worry.' Ray said, `It's OK, Ken, don't worry I'll get you a contract,' but he never did.''

The contract was actually written on the back of a pack of cigarettes, signed by Ullyot and Van Orman who was a constant smoker. There were no monetary terms or even the length of the contract mentioned. Van Orman told Ullyot to pay himself what he needed to live on.

It also turned out to be the only contract Ullyot ever signed with the Komets. Though he was offered other opportunities during the years, including in the NHL, Ullyot never left Fort Wayne. Getting to Fort Wayne took quite a few twists and turns, though.

Ullyot was born June 29, 1921 in Saskatoon, the last of six children – four sisters and two brothers. His father was a businessman who also sometimes ran for political office.

``He was a great man, a very dedicated man,'' Ullyot said.

His mother was a housewife, at least at the start until her husband suffered an asthma attack and died when Ken was five years old.

``In those days they didn't have much for asthma, and this was in 1926,'' he said. ``That of course made my mother the greatest woman in the world. She never complained. She kept the family going.''

She got all the kids off to school, but she couldn't get a job, though she was an accomplished seamstress. Somehow the family made do.

``All those problems were not that noticeable that I paid any attention to them,'' Ullyot said. ``We were never poor, but we never had anything, but neither did anybody else. Nobody had anything, but you didn't know that you didn't have anything because you always had enough to eat, and what the hell more was there?"

When Ullyot turned 16, he quit school to go to work and support his mother, pedaling telegraphs for the Canadian Pacific Railway. Johnny Walker worked for CPR and was about to marry Ullyot's sister so he helped get the youngster a job.

``I didn't know it until later, but I know he did it," Ullyot said. ``You could go in and put an application in and they would put it at the top of the pile. Johnny was the general manager and owned the Saskatoon Quaker hockey club. He had a little pull and he went in and put in a good word for me."

Ullyot pedaled his bike for four years while playing junior hockey.

Almost as soon as he could walk, Ullyot had started skating, learning on the street and then improving to the point where he could compete at the local school. As he grew older, Ullyot was a skinny center with slick passing ability, though he didn't necessarily grow much larger.

``He was tall (6-0), but I don't think he was ever over 150 pounds," said Keith Allen, who played junior hockey with Ullyot and later became a Philadelphia Flyers coach and executive. ``He was a damned good playmaker. He maybe at that stage had some energy in his legs because he used to ride the bike so much. That's probably the strongest his legs ever were."

The team would practice sometimes at 5 or 6 a.m., and the CPR manager gave Ullyot time off to play in the games. Ullyot never dreamed of a professional career, though, in part because eventually he built up enough seniority where he was put in charge the messengers.

He played three seasons with the Saskatoon Quakers starting in 1938, centering a line of Harry Watson and his brother Eddie. Harry Watson eventually played 809 games in the National Hockey League, mostly with the Toronto Maple Leafs. Other players from the team made it to the NHL, including Tony Leswick and Hal Laycoe. They played for the Memorial Cup in the Western Canada finals in Ullyot's final season, losing to eventual champion Winnipeg.

``It didn't matter where they put me, if I got the puck, nobody else could get it," Ullyot said with a chuckle.

But there was some truth to that. The next season, at age 20, Ullyot signed a form tryout contract with the New York Americans who shipped him to play with the Washington Eagles of the Eastern Hockey League. Ullyot had a great season, scoring 27 goals and 76 points, finishing seventh in the league scoring race, but there were other highlights that changed his life.

``I was playing hockey in Madison Square Garden against the New York Rovers, and they stopped the game because somebody bombed Pearl Harbor," he said. ``That was quite an experience. They asked everybody connected to the service to get cracking and get back where they belonged. It didn't look like we would finish the game and then we did. We went home in the train and it was mostly lights out. There weren't any lights on in Washington. We lived about three blocks south of the White House and we had to walk home from the station. It was a pretty scary time for everybody."

There was some discussion for a few days what to do with the rest of the schedule, but it was determined the teams should continue playing. That's pretty much how it went after all the road games.

``We had one bedroom for four of us, and there were times when we'd be on the road and come home at 4 or 5 in the morning," Allen said, ``and the landlady had rented our room out to whomever thinking we wouldn't make it home."

After that season ended in April, Ullyot went home to Saskatoon and immediately joined the Royal Canadian Air Force. He also got married to his girlfriend Violet. They had met one day two years earlier as Vi and her twin sister Vera were walking and a car pulled over to offer them a ride. Riding in the car were Jack Gibson, Ken Wilson and Ullyot.

Ken and Violet went to a dance the next weekend and then dated for two years before getting engaged. Ken wrote from Washington telling her to pick out a ring from the jewelry store she worked at. They were married on August 15, 1942 in Askwith, Saskatchewan, noted, Ullyot says with a grin, for being the center of North America. Wilson was the best man.

``Just about everybody we grew up with got married within two years because they were going into the service and nobody expected to come back," Ullyot said. ``You knew you'd be damn lucky if you came back."

The Ullyots had about 10 days after they were married before he had to leave for Toronto. Vi moved to live with her mother in Vancouver.

Because of repeated dislocations to his right shoulder, Ullyot was not shipped overseas. Or at least that's what he was told originally. After he completed his training in Toronto, Ullyot was awakened one morning by an officer who said he was being shipped out, this time back to Vancouver to work loading planes with ammunition and sometimes repairing the guns.

``They must have figured they better leave Ken on the West Coast because he'll handle the Japs," Ullyot said with a chuckle. ``Lo and behold, when I got there, there were four or five pretty good hockey players, too, who had just been shipped there."

The armed forces had hockey teams all over the country for charitable purposes. Former NHL player and CAF officer Frank Frederickson put together a team and then the Navy and Army did the same on the west coast. The closest Ullyot came to combat was on the ice as the teams would play exhibitions to benefit the Red Cross or Salvation Army, about 20 games a year.

The move was just about perfect for Ullyot because he was reunited with Vi in Vancouver and was never too far away from home.

When the war ended, Ullyot went back to Saskatoon and to work for Canadian Pacific Railroad. He also played for the New Westminster Royals in the Pacific Coast Hockey League and later the Western Hockey League. He led the league in scoring in 1947-48 with 109 points. In 393 career games he scored 193 goals and 467 points. Twice he led the Royals to playoff championships and three times he led them in scoring. When he retired in 1953, Ullyot was the third-highest scorer in league history.

Shoulder injuries basically ended his playing career and started his coaching career. He was 32 years old when he started his first job in Kamloops, British Columbia as a player-coach.

``I don't know if we gave it a second thought that he would become a coach," Allen said. ``It didn't surprise me because he was always a thinking man's hockey player. He had ideas how things should be done and he didn't deviate from his own thoughts."

But there were problems with his first job. His players were guys he had played with and against, and the chemistry was never right. The Elks' record was 27-33-4 and Ullyot was fired after one season.

``They were a little more polite about it and asked me to leave," he said. ``I didn't like being a playing coach. You had a hard time having any control or any authority. Then there were 24 people who were on the board of directors and they were tough to deal with."

He returned to New Westminster that summer and went to work for a friend in the clothing business, which helps explain Ullyot's passion for fine dressing. He was always the best-dressed coach in the International Hockey League.

Ullyot got a couple of coaching offers, and took the one in Prince Albert because he had heard good things about the organization, and it was a farm club of the New York Rangers. Once again Ullyot's brother-in-law Johnny Walker put in a good word. The Mintos liked Ullyot because he was known as a teacher.

Ullyot stayed for four years. His lineup featured future Komets such as Reggie Primeau, Andy Voykin, Bob McCusker, Shorty Melanchuk, Lloyd Maxfield, and Chick Balon. Playing about 50 games a season, the Mintos were 112-75-7 under Ullyot.

``Ken was from Saskatoon, and that team fell apart just about that time, and we got some of those players so they knew of him," Primeau said. ``I had heard of him from playing in New Westminster. I think he was probably about 34, young enough that he could have still been playing."

It was during his time in Prince Albert that Ullyot developed his reputation as a great teacher. He was always finding unique ways to teach his players and get them to think in different ways about the game.

``He was very business-like," Primeau said. ``When he talked, you listened and you understood, too. He was very sharp. He was a good teacher, a strict teacher, but he was good. He taught you things that really meant something, not just simple things. Not many people knew how to do some of those things right, like how to drop a puck right. When you make a drop pass, you don't put a tail on it. You put your stick in front of it and stop it, and I used to take it a little further and if I had time I'd drop it and then fake a shot."

The teaching was also done off the ice as well as on. Ullyot had a big impact on the rest of his players' lives after they retired.

``He was my first coach in 1957," said former Ottawa Senators General Manager Marshall Johnston. ``As a 16-year-old, I have vivid memories of that season. Ken's knowledge of hockey, his teaching ability in fundamentals of the game, and maybe most importantly, his example as a role model at this impressionable time had a lasting influence on my future."

The Mintos listened and improved dramatically as their record steadily got better.

``We had a damn good team every year," Ullyot said. ``We never won any championships, but we had a good team."

The Mintos came close one year. Flin Flon won the Memorial Cup in 1957 but only after winning an epic series against Prince Albert. The series was scheduled for nine games, but a few of the games ended in ties as there was no overtime. A 10th game was needed, and Flin Flon survived before winning the Memorial Cup over Ottawa.

Then Wilson called from Troy in the summer of 1958 to start the next phase of Ullyot's life.

``I said, `Well I don't know if I'm interested or not,' " Ullyot said. ``I have a job here and I'm quite happy with it. It wasn't a lot of money, but it was good money in those days. That was a tough decision."

The chance for ownership is what finally convinced Ullyot to come to Fort Wayne. At the time, Ullyot had two years remaining on a contract in Prince Albert, but Rangers General Manager Muzz Patrick gave his blessing and the Mintos released Ullyot from his contract. He was officially named the Komets general manager on August 12, 1958, and the coach on September 19, 1958.

But once again it was not a great start, and this time it had nothing to do with what happened on the ice. In what almost became an annual ordeal each summer, the International Hockey League needed to find teams to stay alive.

``When I talked to Van Orman in July, they had six teams," Ullyot said. ``I went home to get Vi and the kids, and when I came back there were only three teams.'

Defending champion Indianapolis and finalist Louisville had joined perennial power Cincinnati in dropping out, leaving Fort Wayne Troy and Toledo as the only teams standing. Ullyot, Wilson and commissioner Andy Mulligan hit the road, trying to find new potential partners. They first convinced Indianapolis to return and then talked to the Louisville owner who said he could make it if he could get two players from each team.

The IHL stayed alive with five teams. Ironically, Louisville won the regular season title with Fort Wayne finishing second and then beat the Komets in six games to win the Turner Cup.

The next year the IHL Troy dropped out and Minneapolis, St. Paul, Omaha and Milwaukee were added, but it seemed every summer was a struggle. The league went so far as playing an interlocking schedule with the NHL-sponsored Eastern Hockey League in 1962-63, going against teams such as Hull-Ottawa, Kingston, Syracuse and Sudbury.

Proving no good deed goes unpunished, the following year the EHL plucked St. Paul, Minneapolis and Omaha out of the IHL to form the Central Hockey League. The IHL was left with Fort Wayne, Muskegon and Port Huron before Mulligan convinced owners in Windsor and Chatham to field teams and Des Moines joined the league.

``If it wasn't for the Ken Ullyots of the world and people like him the league probably would have never made it past the first 10 years," current Komets General Manager David Franke said.

To help save money, roster limits were cut from 14 to 12 players. The trainer was the back-up goaltender, playing only in the most extreme circumstances.

``Keeping teams alive was the toughest," Ullyot said. ``You always had to find new teams. You should shut up about bad times because pretty soon everybody starts talking, and then somebody would get scared and say, `I'm leaving.'

``One year (1965) we had six games left with Toledo in the last month and a half and they were going to drop out. We had a chance to win the championship so we had to pay their payroll for the last six weeks. It was on a loan, but you never got it back. The team was owned by a multi-millionaire, and I swear Toledo made money."

The investment paid off as the Komets whipped Toledo in four games during the first round of the playoffs that year before beating Minneapolis to win their second Turner Cup.

Whenever a new building went up, the IHL, EHL and American Hockey League would scramble to see if they could be the first league to get a team in there.

``These things happened all the time with us," Ullyot said. ``Practically every summer we had to find different teams or help somebody out of a problem to keep them alive so we could have a league. All those times we fought to survive because we didn't have another league to go to."

Did the IHL ever come close to folding?

``We didn't think of that. We knew we were going to have a league. We knew we'd come up with something."

Part of that something included Ullyot using his connections in Western Canada to find players for other teams or even loaning them players off his roster. Some of the fans wondered what in the world he was doing, but he was helping keep the league alive so the Komets had someone to play. Sometimes the only way to help the league was by helping another team.

``Survival was our main concern always," he said. ``League problems came ahead of individual problems because we knew if you don't have a league, you can't have a team. We were partners in the league, and you were only as strong as your partners."

Former IHL Commissioner Jack Riley once said, "I know of other times when it looked like some teams were going to go out because of financial trouble, and I'm sure Fort Wayne lent them some money."

Sometimes Ullyot joked that he was a commissioner who coached, too. He often said he could not remember a time when the owners were not concerned about the future of the league.

Another former IHL commissioner, Bill Beagan, said in 1997, "We were very vulnerable, and there's no doubt in my mind the league would have died without them. It's very accurate to say Fort Wayne saved the league in the mid-60s. We would have gone under a couple of times without their help."

The Komets were able to provide that help because Ullyot was able to get things going well on the ice almost immediately upon his arrival in 1958. With returning players such as Eddie Long, Len Thornson, Art Stone and Orrin Gould, former Prince Albert stars Duane Rupp, Larry McLaren and Norm Waslawski and the addition of goaltender Glenn Ramsay from Cincinnati, the Komets were a fun team to watch. More fans than ever came to see them play at Memorial Coliseum.

With the help of business manager Colin Lister, the increased attendance allowed the Komets to play off some critical bills by Christmas of 1958 and Van Orman and Perry rewarded Ullyot with part ownership and he gave Lister a part of it.

The bills were paid off eventually in the middle of the next season, and 1959-60 turned out to be a year for the ages in Komets history. The squad finished the regular season with a 50-16-2 record to set the all-time Fort Wayne record for winning percentage and finish 14 points up in the league race.

Len Ronson scored 62 goals and 109 points, and Len Thornson scored 107 points with Bob McCusker getting 89, Eddie Long 88 and Lloyd Maxfield 78. Rookie and future NHL great John Ferguson struggled in the first half but was a dominating presence in the second half. Goaltender Reno Zanier gave up only 2.61 goals per game.

But that magical season ended in heartbreak. The Komets advanced to the Turner Cup Finals for the second year in a row, this time against the St. Paul Saints. The series was essentially decided in Game 4 that started on April 14 and didn't end until 1:25 a.m. on April 15 in the fourth overtime. The teams almost played two full games before the game-winning goal was scored.

The Komets seemed to have won the game when Long scored with 4:41 left in regulation, but Saints forward Aggie Kukulowicz beat Zanier with a 40-foot slapshot with 2:10 left. The teams battled through one 10-minute and a pair of 20-minute extra sessions to head into the fourth overtime. The Komets had their best chance to win it 55 seconds into the second overtime when Len Ronson was awarded a penalty shot after St. Paul's John Bailey threw his stick at Komet Con Madigan.

Nicknamed ``The Rifleman," Ronson was the perfect player to take the shot, but the puck rolled on him at the last second. Later Thornson hit the post on one side and Ronson later hit it on the other. The Komets hit the post four or five times during the overtimes, Long said.

The goaltenders were spectacular, with the Saints' Glenn Ramsay making 72 saves, including 46 during overtime. Zanier finished with 52 saves, including 28 in overtime. Ullyot had traded Ramsay the summer before because he felt Zanier was better.

The game finally ended when St. Paul's Elliott Chorley scored on a long blast that the far-sighted Zanier never saw. The Komets eventually lost the series in seven games with Chorley scoring three game-winning goals.

It was later discovered Chorley was ineligible. Ullyot, who had asked several times during the series for the league to check Chorley's eligibility, protested at the summer league meetings, and St. Paul's owners offered to return the money but not the championship.

``They had to hear it, and they did, but they wouldn't do anything about it," Ullyot said. ``It broke some of the guys' hearts. I tried to explain it to them. They didn't blame me, but they blamed the league for not checking it closer, and I did, too."

Ferguson later said it was harder to make the Komets that season than it was to make the Montreal Canadiens a few seasons later. He credits Ullyot with developing him into an NHL player.

``Ken is, without doubt, the BEST coach and one of the most knowledgeable people in all of hockey besides being a fine gentleman," Ferguson said.

Ullyot had started teaching almost as soon as he arrived in Fort Wayne. He loved helping players improve, and took great pride in finding different ways to make them think. One day he'd tell the players they had to step onto the ice and head to the left when usually they always went to the right. That way they could learn to start with their off foot if they needed to use it during a game. He'd have players stickhandle the puck while looking up at the scoreboard so they could read him the time, teaching them to keep their heads up.

``I was always trying to teach them the game," Ullyot said. ``The game fundamentally is the same as any other game. You have to know how to do the little things to do the big things. That's the way I look at it. Anybody can skate but not everybody can improve their skating because they don't know what the next step is. A good coach can teach that."

He taught fundamentals every day, but he did it in a way that wasn't boring to the players. He didn't run them through drills just to give them something to do.

``The only time you skated and worked your a-- off was when the coach was hung over," he said, laughing.

Ullyot has always been known for his wickedly dry sense of humor. He once said of Violet, ``When I die, I'm going to be cremated and they're going to spread my ashes at Value City. If they put me in a cemetery I might get to see Violet once a month, but this way I'll get to see her once a week."

He always seemed to have a joke at just the right time. (``That's good, but I don't have one right now," he said.) Ullyot said he picked up his sense of humor from his mother, who could laugh at most things. The players picked up on it and knew they could tease their coach right back. One time Ullyot came to the rink in a foul mood, and defenseman Terry Pembroke said, ``Uh, oh, look out, Vi must have burned the toast this morning."

Instead of steaming, Ullyot busted up laughing.

``I know exactly where I was on the ice the first time I heard Pembroke say it," Ullyot said. ``The first time I heard him say it, everybody was just skating and he was popping off. It was funny and I laughed. I didn't get mad and say shut up. I laughed. Then they started to add a few other little gimmicks to their stuff."

Pembroke said, ``He has the best sense of humor. When he tells stories about himself, they are just classic."

Ullyot said he never told a player to shut up, though he sometimes challenged them to share their witty thoughts with the rest of the team in the locker room.

As a coach, Ullyot was a master psychologist. Sometimes if one player broke curfew, he'd sit the player on the bench, make sure they had a clean towel draped over their shoulders and some water to drink, and then the rest of the team would skate until they couldn't move.

Other times he'd get calls at home telling him which players were out at night so he'd go to practice the next day and ask the players to admit it. The players thought he was omniscient.

``Discipline is part of the game, and you have to make them think about those things," he said. ``I had a lot of little games. I can't remember one guy who made it a habit of coming later or getting on the ice late."

The players respected him and most liked him. Even today, 40 years after some of them quit playing, they regularly call Ullyot to check in, and they used to frequently invite him to golf with them.

``You don't go around looking for it, but it's nice that they think of you," he said. ``I got to love the guys, I really did. We've had a lot of fun with hockey. We've been very fortunate."

They were just as fortunate on the ice. After losing to St. Paul in 1960, the Komets had to start all over again. They finally broke through in

1963. After a brilliant comeback to finish off Muskegon, the Komets beat Minneapolis to win their first Turner Cup.

``It's like, `Hey! This is what I came here for, and I did it,' '' Ullyot said. ``You gain so much knowledge from winning the first one. One thing you realize at our level is you have to worry about injuries when you come into the playoffs. We had a heck of a team two or three times, but the playoffs always have a lot of surprises.''

The Komets lost to Toledo in the finals the next year, but rebounded to beat Des Moines and regain the cup in 1965. Then several of the mainstays started to retire, starting with Long in 1965, Chuck Adamson in 1967, Thornson and John Goodwin in 1968, Primeau, Norm Waslawski and Repka in 1969.

After several stops and starts, Ullyot finally quit coaching in 1970 after he was accused of going onto the ice to take a swing at referee Howie Halter. Ullyot always denied swinging at Halter but admitted going onto the ice. There were no game films back then.

``The devil made me do it,'' Ullyot quipped.

IHL Commissioner Bill Beagan fined Ullyot $500 and suspended him for 30 days (saying the devil made *him* do it). Violet Ullyot told Beagan he added 10 years to her husband's life with the suspension. The two men remain very good friends.

Ullyot finished his career behind the bench with 322 wins and six Turner Cup Finals appearances in eight years. Long said that Ullyot was probably one of the top 100 hockey coaches of all time.

``With great respect to Eddie, I'd say he was in the top 50,'' Beagan said. ``He was a hockey guy, and he understood men. He lived in the skin of a player. He brought the best out of the business people in our league because he emphasized that this was a business. To me, he's the George Halas of hockey in that he's the consummate hockey man.''

To fill his time, Ullyot concentrated on rebuilding the Komets as the general manager, and they won the Turner Cup in 1973, taking eight of nine playoff games.

Ullyot continued to be a major force in the IHL, becoming the lone owner to vote against expanding to Phoenix and Salt Lake in 1984 after the Central Hockey League folded. When he was asked to change his vote so it could be unanimous, Ullyot refused.

``I didn't think the league could handle it yet, and I told them that,'' he said. ``I thought it was a mistake because the costs scared me, the costs of travel. It was nothing personal, but I didn't think it was a good business decision. I wasn't the prophet. I'm not the smartest guy, but I felt as a league we should know what we were doing.''

One of his highlights was signing his son Ron to coach the Komets in 1981. He won 186 games in four years, including 52 in 1983-84.

``To me I don't think it was any different than a guy going to work for his dad in a business,'' Ron Ullyot said. ``Here's somebody who you always admired and idolized and here we had a chance to work together. I know there was a lot of pressure and some people didn't think I had earned it, but I never felt that way. I didn't worry about that. It was exciting to be able to come home and work with my dad.''

Ullyot was just as proud of his daughter Donna who became a nurse at Parkview Hospital and eventually worked with a hospice. She was married to Komets owner David Welker at one time, and her son Billy Welker was the team's stickboy for a while. As an equipment manager, Billy Welker has become one of the most successful men in minor league hockey as his teams have won five championships. He has no bigger fans than his grandparents. The Central Hockey League gave him a lifetime achievement award in 2007.

In 1982 Ullyot stepped down as general manager, but worked for the team until 1985, mostly representing the Komets at league meetings.

``I had just had enough,'' he said. ``I wasn't feeling great and I haven't since. I was kind of relieved because I didn't have to walk in every morning and say, `What was the problem today?' The 80s were very tough.''

In 1997, The Hockey News named Ullyot the IHL's all-time best general manager.

Though he retired in 1985, Ullyot continued to attend virtually every Komets home game until 2004. Even then he'd pester fans, reporters and former players for detailed reports about the team, often offering suggestions that someone, he said, should let the current coach know he could try.

No, Ullyot never got a paper contract from the Komets. It was written on his heart instead, and yes, he was the perfect man for the job.

Coaching

Season	Team	League	GP	W-L-T	PTS	Playoffs
53-54	Kamloops	OSAHL	64	27-33-4	58	*
54-55	Prince Albert	SJHL	47	22-25-0	44	*
55-56	Prince Albert	SJHL	50	33-14-3	69	*
56-57	Prince Albert	SJHL	49	29-18-2	60	*
57-58	Prince Albert	SJHL	51	33-16-2	68	*
58-59	Fort Wayne	IHL	60	32-27-1	65	lost in finals
59-60	Fort Wayne	IHL	68	50-16-2	102	lost in finals
60-61	Fort Wayne	IHL	69	31-35-3	64	lost in semifinals
62-63	Fort Wayne	IHL	70	35-30-5	75	won Turner Cup
63-64	Fort Wayne	IHL	70	41-28-1	83	lost in finals
66-67	Fort Wayne	IHL	72	40-31-1		lost in finals
67-68	Fort Wayne	IHL	72	30-29-13	73	lost in semifinals
70-71	Fort Wayne	IHL		5-8-0	10	*
	Totals		486	264-214-26		

Ken Ullyot's careers statistics Playing Regular season*Playoffs

Season	Team	League	GP	G	A	PTS	PIM	GP	G	A	PTS	PIM
41-42	Washington	EHL	NA	27	49	76	0	*	*	*	*	*
45-46	Saskatoon	WCSHL	Unavailable									
46-47	New Westminster	PCHL	38	23	36	59	10	*	*	*	*	*
47-48	New Westminster	PCHL	64	38	71	109	20	*	*	*	*	*
48-49	New Westminster	PCHL	66	35	41	76	10	*	*	*	*	*
49-50	New Westminster	PCHL	46	23	28	51	14	*	*	*	*	*
50-51	New Westminster	PCHL	70	39	47	86	6	*	*	*	*	*
51-52	New Westminster	PCHL	45	18	21	39	4	*	*	*	*	*
52-53	New Westminster	WHL	64	17	30	47	16	7	3	1	4	2

COLIN LISTER

CHAPTER 6

When Colin Lister was growing up in Perth, Australia, the closest he came to seeing ice outside was when his mother would put a cup of water out overnight during the winter. By morning a little film of ice would be floating on top.

In other words, Lister's background was literally as far away from hockey as person can get on this earth.

Lister left his home in Perth, Australia, at age 20, perhaps figuring he'd be back someday. Instead, Perth and later Australia would never be home again. Lister spent the next several years trying to find a home and a family, bouncing over three continents before finally finding a home, a family and so much more in Fort Wayne.

When Lister was a baby, born July 7, 1927, his father was a salesman for Massey-Harris Tractors and one day his car veered off the road and ran into a picket fence. With part of the fence breaking off and lodging in his skull, and because of the brain damage, his father was never able to work again and infrequently suffered seizures. His mother could sometimes sense the seizures coming and would tell young Colin to run over to the neighbors until she came and got him.

Though almost everything about their lives revolved around caring for the father, Colin did become an avid surfer. Then the heartbreak continued as his mother died of cancer when he was 18.

While working for the Commonwealth Trading Bank of Australia, Lister stayed in Perth for two more years before moving to Sydney where he lived for five years, spending most of his spare time surfing at Bondi Beach in New South Wales. During this period, he also joined a square dancing group called the Denver Dudes. The Dudes were good enough to win a national competition, taking $8,000 in prize money. Lister's share was $1,000 which he spent over three months in a unique way.

``I decided to leave for a `trip around the world,' '' Lister said. ``I traveled through France, Italy, Austria and Switzerland before arriving in London with less than $10 between me and starvation.''

He took a job as a bookkeeper for a garage syndicate that sold and serviced cars in London while living on the famous Baker Street. Then his heart got the urge to wander again, and Lister took a position with the Bank of Montreal. He moved to several locations before settling in Prince Albert, Saskatchewan, a town of about 19,000.

When Lister arrived, he still had a thick Australian accent which the kids teased him about. He decided to break it, but still to this day traces of it can be heard when says things like ``I've bean,'' instead of ``I've been.''

Soon after Lister arrived in Prince Albert, the family he was staying with took him to a hockey game, an exhibition between the New York Rangers and one of their farm teams, the Prince Albert Mintos.

``I fell in love with the game right away,'' he said.

Ironically, he rarely participated in organized sports while growing up but threw himself into hockey and within two months was coaching two teams and was involved with another.

``I read some books, talked to a lot of people and tried to learn doing the job,'' he said. ``Actually, the main thing was they needed somebody to be in charge, and I was willing to give the time.''

Lister also found the other major sporting love of his life while living in Prince Albert. After working at the bank, he would walk home in the late afternoon. Rather than going home to an empty house, he would stop to watch some boys play baseball.

One day there was a group of smaller children playing when one approached Lister to say they needed an umpire.

``But I don't know anything about the game,'' he said.

``If you don't umpire for us, we're going to have to call this game off,'' the boy said.

Lister reluctantly agreed and looked at the catcher to see how the equipment was worn. Though he didn't have a clue what he was doing, Lister stood behind the catcher and called the game. That night on the way home, he stopped at a bookstore to buy a rule book, staying up most of the night reading so he was better prepared the next day.

Around this time, Lister began to serve on the board of directors for the Mintos, becoming acquainted with the team's new coach, Ken Ullyot in 1954. Though he bounced around different banking jobs, Lister stayed involved with baseball and especially hockey.

``I would always take my vacations at training camp time,'' he said.

In the fall of 1958, Ullyot left Prince Albert to become head coach of the International Hockey League's Fort Wayne Komets. The owners told Ullyot the team had lost $60,000 the season before, but the real number was $87,000, and part of Ullyot's deal was that the owners agreed to give him 25 percent of the team if he could quickly pay off a significant portion of the bills.

``The books were in terrible shape, and I only found about half of them,'' Ullyot said. ``I said `I can't do this by myself, I have to have help.' I phoned Colin and asked him if he wanted to come, and he said, `I'll leave tomorrow.' ''

Lister and Ullyot were a remarkable team. Ullyot was the master motivator and teacher of players on the ice, and Lister was an amazing businessman off the ice. Lister never took an honorarium but was always available to speak. The duo met the debt deadline and then did quite a bit better when the Komets reached their first Turner Cup Finals in 1959.

``We paid the big ones off by Christmas,'' Ullyot said. ``We did it by bringing people into the building. We had a hell of a team, and we were traveling by cars and doing everything we could to keep the costs down. I paid myself $125 a week but I did that hoping I could get some stock.''

Ullyot got the stock and gave Lister 5 percent. It eventually grew to 61.5 percent.

At the same time, Lister started getting involved in the local hockey and baseball scenes. He fielded his first baseball team in the Colt League around 1960 with Mr. Komet Eddie Long as his manager. It wasn't until later in his life that Lister's baseball teams achieved some national success, but his 1969 Midget Komets hockey team finished second in the nationals to a team from Detroit that featured Gordie Howe's sons, Mark and Marty.

``His hockey and baseball players became his family," long-time friend Marcia Cuff said. ``He never had a hobby, but he would keep track of all these kids, when they got jobs, got married or had kids he'd write it down in his book. He still gets calls and letters from players who played for him 40 years ago."

There were also a million little things Lister and Ullyot did behind the scenes to help the local youth enjoy the sport. In the late 1950s and early 1960s, kids were using broken sticks they'd gotten from the Komets. Goaltenders were padded with catalogs and phone books and towels, using a first baseman's mitt. There was no place in town to buy equipment and no one had ever heard of sharpening skates. Most players wore adult figure skates and shoved socks into the toes until they fit. Instead of shin pads, players used magazines or soaked and frozen newspapers. Socks were rolled up to protect skinny wrists where work gloves didn't cover.

Then Ullyot and Lister started helping out, requiring Komets to show up at McMillen Park on Saturday mornings. The Komets' old gear would be handed down. Mysteriously, anonymously, the bins at McMillen would fill with new kid-sized equipment each fall.

``Colin and Ken sowed the seeds and fertilized them very well," said long-time Komets statistician Don Detter who was 14 at the time. ``Anything that is going on in hockey in town, kids going to colleges to play or whatever, is due to those gentlemen. It was 100 percent because of them. They would kind of guide things to make sure they were going the right way."

Lister was also a big booster of the Pepsi Komets youth hockey team and served as the general manager for the Northrop High School team for years, even after he was done working for the Komets.

``Colin Lister was the main supporter of the Pepsi Komets for years," former player Rich Stumpf said. ``I remember him sitting in our living room, giving us guidance whenever we ran into a snag, and he traveled on a lot of our road trips."

When the players were done with baseball or hockey, Lister knew it was just the start of their lives. He kept track of all their birthdays and anniversaries and then kept track of their spouses' and kids' birthdays as well. All those players also kept track of him, and many honored Lister by naming their sons Colin after him. The only computer Lister ever used to keep track of all this was the one on top of his shoulders.

While the Komets thrived in the 1960s and early 1970s, so did Lister, becoming the team's face in the business community. There are lots of funny stories about Lister's work with the team.

During a trip to Louisville for an exhibition game in 1959, the Komets woke up the next morning to see a foot of snow on the ground. Three cars took off in different directions and only one made it to Fort Wayne. Lister was riding in one of the cars when it got stuck, meaning they had to trek to safety. While carrying the gate receipts from the night before, Lister grew exhausted and finally lay down in the snow.

``Leave me, leave me," he said weakly.

``We'll leave you," one of the players said, ``but give us the money."

Then they helped Lister up and carried him to a gas station/restaurant where they waited for help.

On January 21, 1970, the Komets ran a promotion allowing any Boy Scout wearing his uniform in for free to watch a game against the Muskegon Mohawks. It was a Wednesday night, so if 2,000 or even 3,000 boys showed up it shouldn't have been a problem. Well, it was a problem because more than 4,000 showed up, sitting and standing anywhere they could fit in, including taking the seats of season-ticket holders.

The announced attendance was 8,537, but there are plenty of people who swear there were more than 10,000 people in the stands that night including the fire marshal who came looking for Lister. He spent the night hiding from the fire marshal in a bathroom and in the Komets training room.

Komets center and Prince Albert native Reggie Primeau had the nickname Hawkeye because of his Cree Indian heritage, but Lister sometimes had another nickname for Primeau.

``He'd pay us in cash in envelopes and he'd put your nickname on it so he'd put Hawkeye or sometimes Running Bear on mine," Primeau said. ``But then when we got into a bad streak and we'd lost a few games, it would just be Primeau on the envelope. I got a kick out of that."

Besides being the face of the team in the business community, Lister also was a contact person for fans during the games. They didn't have to go to him, either.

``He would walk the mezzanine of the coliseum and it would literally take him the whole game to get around because everyone was stopping him and everyone wanted a little piece of Colin's time," said long-time Lister friend and former PGA star Bill Kratzert. ``He just had that charisma and personality that magnetism that you get to experience from few people in your life."

Away from the rink, Lister was often handing out money as he was an easy touch for any of his young players, helping dozens of them buy cars or paying some of their college bills. He once told a friend if he had all the money back he had spent on kids he'd be rich, but he was rich in so many other ways.

``He didn't have a real happy childhood of his own," Cuff said. ``I think what he missed was somebody nurturing him, and he wanted to do that nurturing that he missed as a child. He's the most giving person I've ever known."

One of those kids made the most dramatic change possible in Lister's life. When Robin Bertsch was 16, he was a sophomore catcher at New Haven High School when Lister recruited him to play on the Fort Wayne Komets' Connie Mack team. The two became close friends, and a couple years later, after asking Lister to stand up with him at his wedding, Bertsch asked Lister to attend an Easter service with him at Calvary Temple. Lister had been raised in the Church of England but quit attending when he was 15.

``I knew he didn't have a religious background at all, and I wanted to make sure that he heard the message," Bertsch said. ``I took him that night and afterward we went to the Waffle House on Clinton Street and we sat there and talked."

On March 30, 1975, as they were talking about the moving performance, Bertsch asked, ``Colin, if you died tonight, and you found yourself facing Christ and he asked, `Why should I let you into heaven?' what would be your answer?"

``I honestly wasn't aware of God, even though now I realize that His hand was on me all of those years, and that He was in control even though I didn't acknowledge Him," Lister said. ``I honestly wasn't too thrilled to go to church with Robin, but I said yes because I had a lot of respect for him and probably because I didn't want to disappoint him."

During his high school days, Bertsch had asked some of his friends to consider Christianity with little success. Here was another chance with Lister so he asked the question.

``This is a heavy question for a 47-year-old man who hadn't been in church for over 30 years," Lister recalled. ``I thought fast and started giving him a recital of my `good deeds' and also told him I felt was as good a Christian as many people who go to church. When I was finished, I waited for the pat on the back that I was sure I had earned. Instead this young man looked me straight in the eye and said, `but you haven't answered my question.' "

The pair drove to Lister's apartment where Bertsch pulled out his Bible and started to explain some verses regarding salvation to Lister. Then they prayed together, and, as Lister said, ``That night, in my own apartment, I accepted Jesus Christ as my Lord and Savior.''

``It was unbelievable that it turned out exactly the way I planned it, but it did,'' Bertsch said. ``I allowed myself to be used, and isn't that the best thing a Christian can do? There's nothing I've ever done that has had a more lasting impact. In some ways, whether he knew it or not, God had been working in his heart or it wouldn't have happened.''

Up to that point, Lister had always felt he was living a good life, but now he started living a great one. Unlike some people who become Christians and then wander away, Lister attended church every Sunday. Anyone who knew him saw an immediate change in Lister's life.

``My life took a 180-degree turn, and a whole new dimension was added to my counseling,'' Lister said. ``I began to care much more about people, and can honestly say that I am filled with a true love for my fellow man. Salvation is the most important step, but it is vital to feel a real love for those around us, and to be able to communicate that love to them.''

Former Grace College President John ``Digger'' Davis, who used to be Bob Chase's color man on WOWO's radio broadcasts during the early 1970s, recalls Lister would speak of his new-found faith. He spoke to his teams, at civic luncheons or wherever he was asked. Sometimes Ullyot would question Lister's need for faith, and Lister would respond, ``I'd rather believe and find out I was wrong than not believe and then find out I was wrong.''

``Being a public person, there are many people in that position who would have shrunk from that responsibility or have been embarrassed,'' Bertsch said. ``That was never a possibility with him. He was proud of the decision he had made and wanted to share it. He was always very grateful that I had taken the interest and time to share with him. Maybe he thought that if I hadn't, maybe nobody would have.''

And many people listened.

``His conversion didn't make a catastrophic change because he was already a good person and had high moral standards,'' Davis said. ``I think it deepened a lot of that and put more values on the things he was doing. Colin was not afraid to talk about his faith, and not everybody appreciates that. They think it's a private thing, but that's not Colin. I'm sure there were those who didn't appreciate those conversations."

But many did, and Lister has a legion of close friends.

``Once he turned to Christianity, it was an avalanche of not what he could impose on a person, but the knowledge that he could give the person about Christianity and the Bible in a way that it wasn't intrusive to that person," Kratzert said. ``That's an art in itself. You can certainly have people who have converted to Christianity, but yet they can be overbearing with it and turn the person off that they are talking to. He had the ability to not do that and ride the middle of the road to give you enough or talk to you enough that you would grasp his sincerity and his love for the Lord and the Bible and what it meant to him."

A prime example of how Lister, and God, worked was Jerry Clark who was the Komets' public relations director in the early 1980s. He had been raised Catholic and even entered the seminary, but fell away from the church and God. He had been working for a radio station in Auburn before coming to Fort Wayne.

``Then I moved to the hockey club and here was Colin Lister wearing Calvary Temple and religion on his sleeve," Clark said. ``We used to these great discussions all the time, but I'd always ignore him when it came to religion. Then one day, December 13, 1983, I'm driving down Calhoun Street near South Side High School, and I'm thinking about these recent murders that had taken place there a few weeks earlier, wiping out an entire family.

``I was thinking about this family that had been killed, and this voice of God said to me, `Where would you spend eternity if that happened to your family today?' I started shaking and broke out into a cold sweat, and I drove back and ran into the office, and Colin takes one look at me and says, `What's wrong?' I say, `I need help,' and he immediately knows what I'm talking about."

The men went into a small office to pray and Clark gave his life to the Lord.

``Colin was the person the Lord used to finalize everything," Clark said. ``It had a profound impact on my life."

In fact, Clark and his wife Sandy started attending Calvary Temple and he later became an ordained minister. He now works for The International Fellowship for Christians and Jews in Chicago.

``Colin was there in every major event in my life," Clark said. ``Not a year went by when I didn't receive a card from him on the anniversary of when I received the Lord and on the anniversary of my ordination. Colin was the type, if you were friends, he never forgot you. Only eternity will record the impact that Colin has had on the Kingdom."

Though he never married, Lister has been the best man in nearly 30 weddings and been a groomsman in maybe 40 more. During the summers, he'd have a wedding booked almost every weekend, which sometimes made it a little tough to arrange around baseball schedules.

``He was certainly a person you looked up to and wanted to emulate," said Kratzert, who played for Lister on the Midget Komets and later asked him to be his best man. ``He always handled himself in a professional manner, and he was someone you'd want to copy. As stern as he could be with his instructions on the ice on what he wanted, he could just turn it off after practice and put his arm around you."

Lister took particular pride in helping out young men who came from dysfunctional families. One of those children was Brad Pepple, whose parents were divorced. When he was 12, Pepple would sell pop at the Memorial Coliseum during Komets games. Lister would usually stand in a corner during the games and children would come by to visit.

Shortly after Lister became a Christian, Pepple ran into him at Calvary Temple and told Lister how excited he was to see him there. Lister could not place Pepple's name immediately so he asked a friend.

``He called me at home and invited me to dinner," Pepple said. ``To me it was like George Steinbrenner calling. I was so excited."

Lister became a father figure to Pepple and even identified him as his son in later years. He taught the boy how to shine shoes and how to tie a tie, all the basic things fathers teach sons. Pepple even lived with Lister for about six years through college.

``Here's a kid from a broken family, and he just literally treated me like his own," Pepple said. ``He would drive my 1968 Bel Air and let me drive his Town Car. The other thing I liked about him was that even though he was like a dad to me, he always wanted me to have a good relationship with my parents. That was his wisdom at work."

Besides working for the Komets and running baseball teams, Lister also worked at Calvary Temple on a prayer hotline, volunteering every Sunday from 11 p.m. to 7 a.m. He would sleep when he could, but would answer the phone and pray with the people on the other end of the line.

``I didn't know he worked there, but I had two huge needs in my life," Pepple said. ``One night I was in dire straights and I called the hotline to ask if they would pray for me, and he answered, prayed for me that night, and I just know everything worked out.

``Three or four years later I'm at home and my mom is having problems. I'm all by myself and it's a Tuesday night, and I'm trying to think what I'm going to do. The only thing I knew to do was to call this hotline and guess who answered the phone. Somebody had called in sick and wanted to know if he would cover for them. It was the only Tuesday night he ever worked there and the only Tuesday night I ever called."

Later, Lister helped Pepple by paying some medical bills. Lister did that for a lot of people.

``He was always reaching out," Pepple said. ``I remember specifically this one guy who would call Colin and give him this sad story, and Colin would send him money. I finally told him he was crazy, and the guy wasn't interested in him. He was just always caring in that way, sometimes to a fault."

Lister's easiness with money eventually hurt him badly. The Komets went through many ebbs and flows financially. Before the 1978-79 season, the team faced major debt, but Ullyot was able to secure a loan. That was the season Gregg Pilling coached the team and the Komets pulled through. Before the 1982-83 season the team fell behind another $160,000 but Ullyot was able to secure another loan.

Ullyot eventually retired running the hockey side in 1982, though he was around the business side until 1985. He tried to convince Lister it was time to get out, but Lister had undergone heart bypass surgery and was feeling like he could take on the world. Instead, he took on the world's problems, especially with the hockey team.

``I took over in 1982, which was wonderful timing because that's when Harvester had its problems," Lister said. ``I got out in 1985. We did pretty well for part of the time, but those last three years obviously were a disaster. I got through them and out with nothing. That's the gamble you take, but I thought it was a good gamble at the time. I had a car, an old car, and my clothes and that was absolutely it. I had nothing put away. My checks started bouncing because an attorney put holds on my own personal bank accounts. It was a tough time."

The amazing thing is that Lister could help anyone else with their problems, but he wasn't great about asking for help on his own.

``No one knows how giving Colin was," Kratzert said. ``It was just unbelievable. Colin knew exactly what he was doing and did what he wanted to with his money, and that's the bottom line. He was no fool like some people kind of thought that he was after the Komets were going through all the transitions. That is far, far, far from the truth."

Lister always felt he could find someone to help with the Komets. He could have gotten out and no one would have blamed him, but he hated to see the hockey team die. Instead, a Brinks truck came and took everything in bank safety deposit boxes to Chicago. He was left with his car, his small apartment and some furniture. The debt eventually totaled $280,000, and Lister said the team was worth between $350,000 and $400,000.

``He told me he lost $50,000 three years in a row, and he was the only owner in the league who made his living from his team," Pepple said. ``You look back now and $40,000, $50,000 isn't that big a deal, but back in the 1980s... it just devastated him. They had an offer to sell the franchise once, but Colin said there was no way they were going to sell.

In his mind, it didn't matter what the offer was. He'd have run that up until the day he died if he could have."

``Out of his own need, I saw this man keep giving," Clark said. ``It was infuriating sometimes. I would just go and scream at him, 'Why are you doing this?' He'd say, 'There's hope for them, Jerry.' Every now and then you'd think you were getting through to him, and the next day he'd turn around and do it again."

Cuff remembers one time she and Lister went to visit the Internal Revenue Service.

``They were on his back," she said. ``He didn't have a good attorney. We took trips to the IRS and we didn't know what was going to happen, if they were going to keep him or what."

Actually, IRS officials were delighted to finally have someone from the hockey team to talk to.

Players would sometimes grab their checks on Friday afternoon and rush to the bank to beat their teammates.

``When I first got here that kind of happened," Komets center Ron Leef said. ``The crowds were dismal. It was really the economy at that point that was kind of messing things up. My last year it got kind of rough, but they never missed a paycheck. They talk about the Frankes saving hockey in Fort Wayne, but Colin Lister is the guy who kept it here."

As Derek Ray said, ``It happened to me once where there wasn't enough money to get my check cashed. Colin took care of it immediately. It was scary."

Lister lost the club in 1985, selling the team to Bob Britt. At age 60, after 30 years with the Komets, he was out of hockey, and he underwent another heart surgery but lacked the insurance to pay for it. In 1987 he moved in with Cuff and her mother.

He still had some successes, leading the Northrop High School hockey team, and he continued to sponsor amateur baseball teams, coaching for more than 40 years. His teams won more than 85 percent of their games, but DOX (short for the doctors who sponsored the team) gave him his first National Amateur Baseball Federation World Series appearance in 2002. Lister once estimated he had worked with more than 700 players over the years.

The Northeast Indiana Baseball Association named an award for him, recognizing his ``dedication to the game of baseball and its historic legacy." Other individual honors included being inducted into the Indiana High School Hockey Hall of Fame, the Fort Wayne Baseball Hall of Fame and a Fort Wayne Sports Corporation community service award. He was also named the American Amateur Baseball Regional coach of the year in 2001.

Maybe the two biggest honors came in 2001 when the Komets retired No. 59 (Ullyot was 58 in honor of their Fort Wayne arrival before the 1958-59 season) in his honor and in 2004 the local amateur summer Connie Mack League for high school-aged players was renamed the Colin Lister League.

``You appreciate it, but it is a bit humbling," Lister said. ``I think some of them should have gone to other people. I got at least a couple of them for just being around so long."

That was typical Colin Lister.

``In all those years and all the time I've known him, I've never heard a cross word," Cuff said. ``He's just a happy man in spite of the downs."

Maybe that's because of his faith.

``Young Christians often ask how they can be sure they are doing the right things all the time, and I have a good test for you," Lister once said in a speech. ``If you feel the slightest doubt about whether you should be involved in that particular activity or place, just ask yourself, if the Lord were to return at that very instant, you would be proud or ashamed... you will have your answer."

There are not many things in life that Colin Lister needs to be ashamed of.

``If you as a man or woman can go through life and meet someone like Colin Lister and have them be in your life for the period of time I've had him in my life, you have to consider yourself a very lucky person," Kratzert said. ``There are only going to be four or five of those people at most in a normal lifetime. That's how I look at Colin Lister."

LIONEL REPKA

CHAPTER 7

Maybe no Komet has been better prepared for his post-hockey career than Lionel Repka. That's partly because he was able to fold hockey and the Komets into his profession. He probably signed more autographs after he retired than he did as a player.

By the time Repka retired at the end of the 1968-69 season, he had already worked for two summers selling insurance policies. With the help of Komets owners Ken Ullyot and Colin Lister, Repka would send out letters each summer to season-ticket holders asking for appointments.

``I used to send out a letter saying, `Old hockey players never die, some become good insurance investment advisors which is what I want to do when my career is over,' '' Repka said. ``And then I'd end with, `and I'll be calling you in a few days.' ''

He sent out a few and before he knew it, he was setting up evening interviews. He always tried to set up three meetings each night. He was always comfortable talking to couples around their kitchen table or in their living rooms, which is how insurance was sold in those days, but there was one little problem.

``You know what, all we'd talk about was hockey and the Komets,'' he said. ``Then before I know it, I'm late for the other appointment. After about a month, I haven't sold anything and things are getting kind of tight. I'm actually failing at the business because I didn't have a chance to give my presentation.''

So Repka changed his tactics, sending another letter telling folks they would get a free official Komets puck when they met if they could tell him what 18,786 means. People tried guessing square inches on the ice, penalty minutes or things do to with insurance policies.

``It had nothing to do with insurance or hockey, but I'd tell them it could be one of the most significant numbers in your lifetime," Repka said. ``That perked up their ears, and I give them the hockey puck."

The number represented the number of meals a person had to buy after age 65 if they lived the normal life expectancy. He added expenses such as water and electricity to build that number to $200,000 and then asked the couple what they had done to prepare for that $200,000.

``Then I'd bring out my flip chart and I'm right into it," Repka said. ``Before you know it, I tell my story and boom, I am selling. It was amazing how that worked. The thing was, I had the people to see and I was trying to learn the skills, but this hockey thing would drive me nuts. I couldn't get any interviews going, but as soon as I gave them the hockey puck they were happy."

And he was happy. The business got to be so strong that Repka retired in 1969 at age 34 because he could make more money selling insurance and mutual funds.

Like many of his teammates when they came to Fort Wayne, Repka never expected it to become home, but each time he has faced a crisis in his life, the city has always taken care of Repka and his family.

Leaning forward, his eyes flashing, Repka can't wait to tell what Fort Wayne has meant to him.

``Can I say it in one word?" he says. ``Everything."

Repka said he'd like to know how many former players have retired and stayed in other Midwest hockey cities such as Indianapolis, Toledo, Port Huron or Muskegon. He's guessing Fort Wayne might have more former players than all of those cities combined.

``After everything, we just knew this was the place to stay," he said. ``Let me put it this way, Fort Wayne is our security blanket. I think most of the guys feel the same way."

``Part of it is our children were born here," Repka's wife Helen said. ``That sort of made it home. We moved around several years before we came here so we were ready for something to be home. It's where our heart is."

In many ways, Repka was born with the heart of the lion he was named after. He was born February 7, 1935 in Vilma, Alberta, but it seemed unlikely he would survive for very long. No matter how much Jack and Emily Repka prayed, for some reason, the unnamed baby could not keep his food down and he continued to weaken. After a few weeks, a priest performed the last rites.

But then one day, for some unknown reason, the baby started to digest his food. As he became stronger, Emily Repka was reading through a name book when she came across ``Lionel" which meant young lion.

Lionel was the oldest of five children with two brothers and two sisters. His father was a physical education instructor and his mother a housewife.

He started skating at age 5 and though he lived out on the ice, Repka never played organized hockey until he was 14.

``Vilna was a little town and we didn't have enough players to make a team," Repka said. ``It was a farming community, and most of the kids were bussed in or they drove in for school. We never had a team so we just played for fun."

Today, Repka would probably be too far behind the other kids to dream of becoming a professional player, but it was a different time.

Because his father got a promotion when Repka was 14, the family moved to Edmonton and Lionel started playing organized hockey. Partly because he was a good skater, he started as a left wing where he stayed until junior hockey. While playing with the Edmonton Oil Kings in junior hockey, Repka was moved to defense when coach Ed McAuley made some changes to cover for three injured defensemen.

``So the coach put me on defense, and before you knew it, I just stayed there," he said. ``I was happy because I was playing a lot. I was on the second line as a left winger and we had three lines, but the defensemen played every second shift. When I look back at it now, I think playing left wing helped me handling the puck and with power plays and such later."

Then he caught a break when the Regina Pats won the West playoffs for the Memorial Cup. They were allowed to pick up three extra players and brought Repka in to play defense. That meant he took his first airplane trip.

Around that time, Repka attended the party of a friend and met Helen Bolte. They were 19, and he says it was love at first sight. It turned out their best friends were dating and would later marry. He was actually dating someone else at the time, and she had dated a couple of hockey players previously.

``I thought he was a rascal," she said, laughing. ``He was a lot of fun, but he was a rascal."

They dated four years while Lionel played and Helen continued her education to become an x-ray technician. They were married May 18, 1957 in Edmonton.

Repka's career continued to progress and in 1955 he went to training camp with the Detroit Red Wings. Then he and teammate Al Arbour were sent back to Edmonton where the coach was future International Hockey League Commissioner Bud Poile. The next year Repka was one of several players moved to the Seattle Americans where Keith Allen was the coach. The following year future Komets coach Marc Boileau joined the team.

But then a major shoulder injury and surgery sidelined Repka in 1958-59. He didn't start feeling better until near the end of the season, he had nowhere to play.

``The IHL season went a month or two longer, and I got a phone call asking me if I'd like to come to Fort Wayne," Repka said.

Allen, who was one of Fort Wayne coach Ken Ullyot's best friends, talked Repka into giving the Komets a chance. While Helen remained working in Edmonton, Lionel was met at the airport by Ullyot and Lister.

The Repkas were quickly reunited under terrible circumstances. Repka's brother Ron was an extremely talented man wrote jingles for radio stations and led a 14-piece orchestra. The group was returning from a performance in Calgary one night when a driver coming the other way fell asleep at the wheel and crossed over the center line to start a massive wreck.

Believing he only had a broken leg, Ron Repka told rescue workers to take everyone else to the county hospital first. He arrived eventually and was placed on a gurney in the hall.

``Then the Royal Canadian Mounted Police came to the house to let my mom and dad know what happened," Lionel said. ``By the time they got there the next day, he was already in deep shock and dying from a ruptured spleen. There was nothing they could do for him."

Lionel left the Komets to return for the funeral. His season was over after 15 games with three goals and five points, but Ullyot had seen enough to know he wanted Repka back.

``I remember Ken said to me, `If you ever need a job, there's one here for you,' " Repka said. ``I hoped he meant it because nobody ever said that in those days, but I also believed him. There were no such things as agents or anything, and I remember when he said that I just thought, `Wow!' Ken was real good about that kind of stuff."

Repka said he considered not coming back the next year, getting an offer from Victoria of the Western Hockey League, but he had already become good friends with Komets such as Eddie Long, Len Thornson and Lloyd Maxfield among others.

``Sometimes it's who you play with and how the guys are and the coaching and the atmosphere in the dressing room that can make all the difference," he said.

All those things made a tremendous difference in 1959-60 as the Komets put together a season for the ages, blitzing through the International Hockey League with a 50-16-2 record. Repka was teamed with Duane Rupp as the Komets set all sorts of records for wins, winning percentage, goals for and goals against.

``It's funny how you can communicate with a guy, and Duane and I had that," Repka said. ``And we had such powerful forwards to work with."

The Komets had an amazing defensive quartet of Con Madigan, Andy Voykin and Rupp and Repka. They were great all-around players.

``That defense was the best you've ever seen," Long said.

That included Repka who had an amazing rookie season with 9 goals and 46 points in 68 games. All four of the defensemen earned more than 40 points, led by Madigan's 57.

``In those days we didn't have offensive defensemen," Thornson said. ``The first thing that was brought up back in those days when you played defense was that you were a defensive defenseman. Lionel and Madigan were both tremendously good offensively as well as defensively."

The season ended in heartbreak as the Komets lost to St. Paul in the Turner Cup Finals. Even nearly 50 years later, the loss still stings Repka.

``We should have won the whole d--- thing," he said. ``You wouldn't believe how good that team was. In fact, we couldn't believe we had lost. The thing I remember the most out of all the playoffs is that one we lost more than the ones we won. It was just so devastating."

That was also the year of the longest game in Komets and IHL history as Fort Wayne battled St. Paul through four overtimes in a game that started on April 14 and ended on April 15, 1960. And that's where the problem starts. St. Paul tied the game with 2:10 left in regulation on a 40-foot slap shot by Aggie Kukulowicz past Komets goaltender Reno Zanier who always had problems on long shots because of poor eyesight. As the game dragged on and on, three hours later an exhausted Kukulowicz told an off-ice official he wished he had never scored the goal.

Both teams had chances to win during the first three overtimes, but play continued until 1:25 a.m. when St. Paul's Eliot Chorley rifled a slap shot from the blue line that hit Zanier's stick and deflected into the net.

``I remember that puck going up in the air," Repka said. ``It hit somebody's stick and went up and over us and hit Reno on the back. I was maybe 15-20 feet from the net. It was one of the flukiest goals ever.

``I remember I got home about 2 in the morning. We had just finished and I was hot. I opened a bottle of beer and lay back, and I honestly didn't have the strength to pick it up and drink it. Everybody was wiped out."

Trailing the series 3-1, the Komets rallied to force a Game 7, but St. Paul won 3-1. The Komets' disappointment tripled when they found out a few weeks later that Chorley, who scored three game-winning goals in the series, should have been ineligible to play. At the time the IHL was considered an amateur league and all transactions had to be cleared through the Central Registry in Montreal. The Komets called to check on Chorley before the series, but could never get an answer and figured the Saint had been cleared to play. After all, the IHL was allowing him to play.

The loss haunted the Komets for several seasons, and it took them a while to regroup and come back to win Turner Cups in 1963 and 1965.

``Our hearts were broken," Repka said. ``That one broke a lot of our spirit. As good as we were, it still…"

The depressed Komets struggled after that, losing in the semifinals in 1961 and failing to make the playoffs in 1962. Then Ullyot kicked re-tooling the team into high gear, bringing in such players as Bobby Rivard, Norm Waslawski, Roger Maisonneuve, Nellie Bulloch and goaltender Chuck Adamson.

Off the ice, Lionel and Helen welcomed son Ron in 1961 and David in 1963. While the Komets were playing a game in Indianapolis, Helen went into labor and Vi Ullyot took her to Parkview Memorial Hospital. Rushing home, Lionel arrived just as the nurses were taking Ron out of the delivery room to clean him up.

It was during the early 1960s that Repka started to blossom offensively with Ullyot's encouragement. He'd take the puck in his own zone and charge up ice with organist Jack Loos playing the ``Choo Choo" music as Repka tore up ice on another rush.

``Lionel always had a strong personality and he tried to enjoy the game to its fullest," Ullyot said. ``He loved the game. He was very confident and he let everybody know it. I let him play his own game, and he didn't disappoint me.

``And he played well everywhere, no matter what building we were playing in."

Repka scored 47, 34, 54 and 56 points over his next four seasons. Then he really kicked it up with 67 points in 1964-65 and a league-record 80 in 1965-66. During this time he was paired with Cal Purinton, Terry Pembroke and Roger Galipeau. Though he played with different partners, usually rookies, almost every season, Repka was consistent and smooth each game. He was the Komets' backbone on the blue line.

``And he had a tough time seeing because one eye has some problems in it," Long said. ``He was deceiving, too. He was stronger than a lot of people thought he was. He hung around and we had a good, top defenseman for years."

Repka was named all-IHL in 1960, 1964 and 1965, winning the Governor's Trophy as the league's top defenseman in 1965.

During this time, Repka forged friendships that have lasted him a lifetime with Komets such as Purinton, Reggie Primeau, Long, Thornson and Gerry Randall among others.

He recalls one particular story from 1963 after Helen had taken the boys home to Edmonton to see her ailing mother. The Repkas were renting a home on Tennessee Avenue from a woman who went to Florida in the wintertime.

``After practice one day I happened to mention that I wanted to surprise Helen by getting the living room and kitchen painted before she got back," he said. ``I was telling Reggie and Cal that I was hoping I could get it done, and before I knew it, they were there to help me. I still remember them taking scarves and towels and putting them over their heads because we were doing the ceilings.

``That's just the way it was with all of us."

That camaraderie carried over on the ice where the Komets' familiarity with each other was a huge advantage. In the era when teams played with only 12 or 14 skaters, they had at least half the team returning each season.

``We had three really good center-icemen in those days in Lenny, Reggie and Bobby (Rivard)," Repka said. ``They used their defensemen very well, and Rivard would play the other point on the power play. After playing together for so long, you just knew each other very well and you had confidence in the other guy."

Then in 1966 Repka decided to retire to try a donut franchise business in Seattle. The last thing Ullyot told Repka before he left was that there was a job waiting for him if he needed it. Just when the business was at its very worst, Ullyot called again and encouraged Repka to return to Fort Wayne.

``There is an old saying I heard when I was a teenager, 'Whether a man has a nest egg or a goose egg all depends on the chick that he marries,' " Repka said. ``Helen never scolded me or did anything but support me because I was the one who did the whole thing."

After returning to Fort Wayne, Repka scored 38 points in 1967-68 and 40 in 1968-69. During his spare time, he worked on acquiring his securities license and selling insurance in the summers.

He finally retired in 1969 to continue what has become a lucrative business. He had played 740 games over 11 seasons, scoring 98 goals, 437 assists and 535 points. He ranks second to Jim Burton among all-time Komets defensemen in points. His No. 6 jersey was retired by the Komets on January, 26, 1991.

``The thing I was most happy about was getting off the bus," Repka said. ``I missed the guys, and I missed playing, but I didn't miss getting on that bus and coming home at 2 and 3 in the morning."

``My concern was that he wouldn't miss hockey so much," Helen said. ``I just wanted him to be able to adapt. Some of the players who retire have a tough time adjusting, and it wasn't for him. He was already selling insurance and knew what his future was."

With the Komets' help and his good name, Repka got a great start selling small group health plans. It was so successful he had to hire extra help because he couldn't handle everything. His daytime requirements increased dramatically when Repka became involved with business owners and partnerships.

``I made as much in one deal as I did in an entire year playing hockey," Repka said. ``We just didn't make too much when we were playing in that era. It was just how the industry was at that time. You played because you loved it.

``After that first failure I was determined to succeed the second time. My mental outlook was different. Helen helped me in that she believed in me."

Then he opened Repka and Associates, and later his sons went into similar fields with Ron getting into pension plans and David into investments, managing a mutual stock fund of his own. The business was successful and Repka was able to retire in 1997 at age 62, though he still kept his hand in through his sons.

In 1994 the Repkas bought a home in Gold Canyon, Ariz., where they spend the winters.

During the summer of 2001, Repka experienced a blessing from his playing days he never could have expected. That summer he was contacted by fan Randy Dannenfelser who grew up in New York idolizing Repka.

In 1959 Dannenfelser's mother had died of a stroke, and he was living with his aunt and uncle. He found some solace in listening to Komets games on WOWO from Bob Chase, and Repka was his favorite player because he was also a defenseman.

Over the 1961 Christmas break, Dannenfelser wrote his hero. Figuring he might get a response if he included a question, he asked what number Repka wore. As a kid he had hope, but he was still somewhat depressed and didn't know whether to expect a response.

Repka's letter and an autographed picture arrived on March 8, 1962.

``Thank you very much for your letter which I received last week,'' Repka's letter on Komets stationery began. ``Glad to hear that you follow the Komets over WOWO and enjoy playing hockey with your three friends.

``As to your question about my hockey number, Randy, you are right. I wear number 6. I am also an alternate captain like you are on your hockey team.

``We are hoping to make the playoffs this year. So far we are in fifth place.

``Thanks again Randy for your interesting letter.''

Dannenfelser was so thrilled he wasn't sure how he opened the envelope without ripping it.

``It was the first time that I can remember since my mother died that I experienced elation,'' he said. ``It made me feel very, very special. I couldn't believe a great hockey player took the time to write to me. After that I experienced elation and great joy as kids normally do when they grow up. It seemed to throw my emotions back into balance.''

The next day his aunt replaced No. 2 with No. 6 on his uniform.

Almost 40 years later, Dannenfelser was looking up Komets statistics on the internet when he decided he should try using the internet to contact. He wanted to thank Repka for the letter and let him know how much it meant to him as a boy. He wrote a three-page letter.

``When I first started reading, it brought back memories of when I was 12 or 13 and how thrilled I was with my idols,'' Repka said. ``This brought tears to my eyes. It just made me feel very good.''

A few days later the men talked by phone for three hours, becoming fast friends. Then a few months later Repka called Dannenfelser and told how his son Ron had died Sept. 18, 2001, when he was hit by a car while riding a bike.

``My heart is absolutely going out to him, trying to think of a way I could give back a little to him what he gave me back in 1962," Dannenfelser said. ``We've kind of reversed roles. I don't know what he's going through, but I do have some ideas what his grandsons are going through. I know Lionel is a man of deep faith, and I thank God for that."

David Repka and Ron's widow Sharon helped start the Ronald G. Repka Foundation, a nonprofit foundation to promote bicycle/motorist safety awareness, building bicycle trails, youth sports and cancer support. Besides an annual fundraising golf tournament for the foundation, Helen discovered some artistic ability later in life and uses it to design bookmarks and note cards for the foundation and cancer support. To benefit the foundation, Dannenfelser's wife Barbara created a Komets quilt that showed all the team's logos through the years. After its first six years, the foundation continues to grow to support a broad range needs in the Fort Wayne community.

``I'm getting paid back tenfold for what I gave him," Repka said. ``I'm grateful and also humbled. You just never know how you touch people's lives."

That's kind of the way Fort Wayne has touched the Repka family, never forgetting Lionel ``Choo Choo" Repka.

One day a few years ago, Repka's grandson Steven met one of his Homestead High School teachers who asked if he was related to Lionel Repka. After telling the teacher Lionel was his grandfather, the teacher said, ``He was one of the best hockey players in Fort Wayne history."

Steven later told the story to his grandmother.

``We're so grateful that our sons were born here and we decided to stay in Fort Wayne," Lionel said. ``Everything we have is because of Fort Wayne. It isn't anything I did or Helen did, it's just because this city has always been a strong, traditional family community."

Lionel Repka's careers statistics

Season	Team	League	GP	G	A	PTS	PIM	GP	G	A	PTS	PIM
					Regular season					Playoffs		
55-56	Edmonton	WHL	68	5	12	17	54	3	0	0	0	0
56-57	Seattle	WHL	61	6	15	21	45	6	0	2	2	6
57-58	Seattle	WHL	66	1	12	13	81	9	0	0	0	0
58-59	Spokane	WHL	32	1	5	6	24	*	*	*	*	*
58-59	Fort Wayne	IHL	15	3	2	5	14	*	*	*	*	*
59-60	Fort Wayne	IHL	68	9	37	46	90	13	3	2	5	19
60-61	Fort Wayne	IHL	66	11	36	47	48	8	0	3	3	4
61-62	Fort Wayne	IHL	61	10	24	34	53	*	*	*	*	*
62-63	Fort Wayne	IHL	70	5	49	54	61	11	1	11	12	8
63-64	Fort Wayne	IHL	68	7	49	56	58	1	0	0	0	0
64-65	Fort Wayne	IHL	70	10	57	67	83	10	2	6	8	12
65-66	Fort Wayne	IHL	70	13	67	80	55	6	0	4	4	2
66-67	Fort Wayne	IHL	44	6	19	25	18	13	3	6	9	18
67-68	Fort Wayne	IHL	64	8	30	38	68	6	1	4	5	15
68-69	Fort Wayne	IHL	70	8	32	40	94	6	0	1	1	6

*Playoffs

REGGIE PRIMEAU

CHAPTER 8

Reggie Primeau was 24 years old when his National Hockey League dream died. With their three children in the back seat, he and his wife Sonja were driving across the country from Portland, Oregon, when they got as far as Cheyenne, Wyoming, in January, 1961. Primeau had just been released by the Western Hockey League's Portland Buckaroos after the Boston Bruins had sent center Larry Leach out on a rehabilitation assignment. Primeau was expendable.

At that time he felt like his career was expendable. The Primeaus decided to stay overnight and call their friend Bruce Walker in Denver to ask him to come up for a short visit to talk things over. After bouncing around the minors through six teams in four years and never playing more than 57 games in one spot, Primeau was wondering if it wasn't time to try the next phase of his life. This one sure wasn't working out.

``I had worked at the brewery over the summers and thought I might be able to catch on there," he said.

There was an offer from his former Prince Albert junior coach Ken Ullyot to play for the Komets, but Cheyenne just happened to be at the intersection where the Primeaus could turn North and head directly home.

``It was kind of hard because Pam was just a baby at six months, Mitch was three and Greg was two," Sonja Primeau said. ``There was no such thing as disposable diapers back then, and the money was tight. It was tempting just to go home, but in the wintertime there probably wouldn't have been as much to do up there."

Instead of heading home, Primeau talked with Walker and then called home to talk to his mother. Mary Catherine Primeau had given birth to 16 children and raised 12. Reggie was the second youngest.

``I told her where I was and what I was thinking," he said. ``She said, 'No, Reg, don't quit, keep going and stay with this.' So I kept going and I got here. Once I made up my mind, that was it."

Primeau went on to become one of the Komets' all-time best players and a two-time Turner Cup champion. He also became a Fort Wayne institution. Getting there was the tricky part.

Reggie Primeau was born in Prince Albert, Saskatchewan, on August 13, 1936, the sixth of seven boys along with five sisters. His oldest brother, Alex, was 20 when Reggie was born. Their father, Richard Primeau, worked for the city, which had a population of about 19,000. He'd plow the snow in the winter, run the city pool in the summer and pull the horse team that graded the streets any time in between.

Mary Catherine worked in the house, cooking for all the children, and was heavily involved with the church and quilting.

The Primeau boys all played sports. Ernie was considered a prospect until he fought in World War II.

``They tell me when he came back he wasn't the same as a player because of the five years," Reggie said.

He grew up playing hockey in the streets with a tennis ball, playing under the street lights after dark. Then the Sicks Brewery opened an open-air rink and allowed the children to play for free. The only stipulations were no fighting and no cursing.

``It was only about a block from our house, and I would see the lights go on after supper," he said. ``As soon as the lights went on, I was gone. I was able to play there when I was about six or seven years old. I remember it had square corners. I always tell everybody that's how I got my nose because I couldn't turn in the corners."

He'd play there after school from 4 to 6 p.m. before coming home to bring in the wood and eat. Then he'd go back from 7 to 9 p.m. There would be skating one night and hockey the next, but he was on the ice every night.

Primeau said he was a decent student but he could have been better if he wasn't always thinking about hockey or baseball. He was always thinking about whom he was going to play against and what he needed to do. He knew right away he wanted to be a professional player. After a school reunion a few years ago, a classmate wrote, `` When I speak about our reunion, I feel Reggie you were the most successful there. You followed your dream. The rest of us were too afraid to get out of the mainstream."

Fortunately, he was blessed with a speedy legs and quicker hands. He also liked to work hard.

Because he signed a tryout contract with the New York Rangers, Primeau joined the Prince Albert Mintos of the Saskatchewan Junior Hockey League at age 16, skipping from midget to juniors. The next year the Mintos had a new coach, Ken Ullyot.

``There were so many things that he taught, like always keeping your head up," Primeau said. ``He liked me to shoot, and I didn't shoot an awful lot. I was a center so I was supposed to pass, and he used to give me heck for not shooting. He always said I should have shot when I would look to pass because I was dead center on the net, but if I could see someone from out of the corner of my eye, I'd give it to him and take the assist."

Ullyot drilled the Mintos constantly. Sometimes it became monotonous, especially since the coach was very particular about how things were done. He was particularly hard on Primeau because he knew how good the scrappy center could be. One time, Primeau said he even wanted to slug Ullyot.

``I said, 'Oh, I can't play for him any more,' " Primeau recalled. ``I was still young, but then I'd go to the Rangers camps and I could do all the drills. Everything they did, I could do because we practiced them so much. Then it changed. A couple of us said he was tough, but then we were happy that he was."

Ullyot chuckles when he hears that story today.

``I have all the respect in the world for Reggie," he said. ``He learned the game very fast, and he had so much fun with the game. I always kind of hoped Reggie would be a good coach."

Later in Fort Wayne, Ullyot would use Primeau to demonstrate the drills for the new players.

When he was 18, Primeau was playing in a baseball tournament in Birch Hills, Saskatchewan, about 40 miles from Prince Albert. During a break between games and hoping to get something to eat, he jumped into the back of a pick-up truck that was heading into town. That's when he met Sonja who was in the back of the truck with a couple friends. She was his first and last girlfriend.

``We played in the league there so we were back in Birch Hills a few times," he said.

She was only 16.

``In those days 40 miles seems like a long way, but we wrote letters back and forth," she said. ``Later I ended up working at the Saskatchewan Government Telephone as a long distance telephone operator. It was just a job I got right after high school."

They got married December 10, 1956, in Prince Albert the·year before he turned pro. Children Rich, Greg, Pam and Rodney followed and now the Primeaus have seven grandchildren.

Primeau remained the Rangers' property for about six seasons, but he could never get to New York. Instead, they sent him everywhere, to Saskatoon, St. Paul, Troy and Trois Rivieres, Greensboro, Milwaukee and Portland.

He even ended up briefly with Springfield of the AHL. Because the Falcons were on a road trip, Primeau practiced with all-time great player and nutcase Eddie Shore.

``He did some weird things like asking me how I tied my skates," Primeau said. ``When I came in the dressing room, I started getting nervous."

Shore showed Primeau an impractical way to tie his skates so they could be removed quickly in case he suffered a foot or ankle injury. He also showed him something practical by asking Primeau how he took a shot. As Primeau mimicked a shot, Shore checked him across the shoulder to knock the center off-balance. Then he showed Primeau how to shoot with his knees bent so he couldn't be knocked over as easily.

``He taught me a good lesson, because when I did get in front of the net later on I'd bend my knees," Primeau said.

Because the Falcons already had enough players, Primeau asked to go where he could play and was sent to Troy of the International Hockey League where he played 29 games, scoring 19 points. The next season He started out with seven games in Greensboro of the Eastern Hockey League before getting traded to Milwaukee where he led the Falcons with 39 goals and 90 points in 57 games.

When the Falcons folded in November of 1960, the Komets acquired Primeau's rights, but he was already playing with Portland, scoring 10 points in 28 games.

``He was hard to get because everybody wanted him, but I was smarter than the rest of them," Ullyot said. How? ``I can't give out things like that."

Actually, Ullyot asked his wife Violet to talk to Primeau, and that did the trick.

By the time the Primeaus got to Fort Wayne, Ullyot already had former Mintos Lloyd Maxfield and Andy Voykin playing for the Komets. There were also several other players from around the Saskatoon area.

Primeau centered a line of Jim Baryluk and Maxfield, scoring 25 points in 27 games and leading the Komets in the playoffs with 11 points in eight games. The next season he was the team's second-leading scorer with 105 points.

By then, Fort Wayne had become home because the kids were entering school. Finally, Primeau had found a hockey home. As quickly as he became the best skater on the team, the fans took to him. They got some help from organist Norm Carroll. Recognizing Primeau's Cree heritage from his mother's side of the family, Carroll would sometimes play an Indian ``war dance" before Primeau would take a faceoff.

``It would get me going, too," Primeau said with a laugh.

Andy Voykin had called Primeau Hawkeye during their junior days because of the book, ``Last of the Mohicans." It was also because Primeau was so sharp in front of the net. Then Roger Maisonneuve started calling Primeau ``Chief."

Ullyot even got in on the act, saying, ``I've known him since he was born and was the first one into the teepee to change his diaper."

Primeau was everything Ullyot liked in a center. He could skate, shoot, play defense and especially, pass. He could also be very sneaky.

``Say I'm the opposition and I'm stickhandling and trying to get away, and Reggie is behind him but he can't see him," Lionel Repka said. ``Reggie would tap his stick and say, 'Back, back, back.' The guy would pass it back to Reggie. Or else he'd say 'Boards, boards' and the guy would pass the puck off the boards. Another time a guy got the puck and was headed up ice, and Reggie is trailing behind and taps his stick on the ice and goes 'Wayne, Wayne.' The guy saw what happened and said, 'That's not fair, he used my name!' Reggie could cheat like that."

Ullyot used Primeau's savvy and previous experience with him as an example for the rest of the team. One day he asked the players if they knew who the seventh player on the ice was for each team. Only Primeau knew Ullyot was talking about the boards and then Ullyot used Primeau to demonstrate.

``He's a leader on the ice by what he does," Ullyot said. ``He was one of those players who could get on the ice and within two minutes of instruction know exactly what to do. When it worked, it just thrilled me to death. You don't bring it out or make them do it, you have to depend on their talent for them to show it when it was needed. Reggie could do that and he loved playing with Norm and Roger. He loved those two guys because they could shoot. He always liked to make that perfect pass."

Along with wingers Norm Waslawski and Roger Maisonneuve, Primeau helped give the Komets a lethal second line scoring option. In 1962-63, Primeau scored 36 goals and Waslawski and Maisonneuve 35 each. Their most important goals came during the playoffs that year as the Komets finally broke through and won their first Turner Cup after losing in the finals in 1959 and 1960. Primeau scored five goals and Maisonneuve six during the postseason, and Waslawski led the Komets with nine.

Their finest fete was combining to help the Komets overcome a 6-1 deficit in Muskegon to clinch the semifinal series. Waslawski won the game in overtime.

``It was like 6-1 late in the second period but we got a goal," Primeau said. ``We came into the locker room and just said we had nothing to lose. We just kept nibbling away at it. That was a lot of fun."

Many Komets feel they won the Turner Cup with that victory because they felt invincible after that.

``When they came back, that was the biggest thrill," Ullyot said. ``We won a lot of tough games when we came from behind, even on the road. Reggie's line was playing so well, they could stick-handle down the main street in Muskegon and the public couldn't have stopped them."

Primeau always performed well in the playoffs.

``When the playoffs would come, there was always a song that would get me going and fired up," Primeau said. ``I'd always listen to that on the way to the rink. You're always so nervous, it's a good feeling, but you are always ready to go. It's just a wonderful feeling."

It was a wonderful feeling again in 1965 as the Komets regained the cup after losing to Toledo in the 1964 finals.

After getting a great job offer that included a car, Primeau decided to retire after the 1965 season. He finally decided he had made a mistake and came back for the final 27 games of the 1965-66 season, quickly regaining his form to finish with 31 points. He retired again after that season, but once again came back for 1967-68, this time scoring 80 points in 72 games.

The only problem was Primeau had suffered a serious knee injury at the end of that season. He came back the next season, 1968-69, scoring 50 points in 55 games, but he knew something was wrong.

``The doctor told me I wouldn't ever play again, but tried to play and I went out and skated," he said. ``Someone passed the puck and I tried to stop it with my skate and it went right through. My knee was shot. I tried to play and I finished that year but I wasn't as strong."

Primeau's Komets totals are 222 goals, 373 assists and 595 points in 511 games. If he had maintained his regular pace during the season-and-a-half he missed because of retirements, Primeau would probably rank among the Komets' top five all-time in terms of goals, games and points, but instead he's 15th in goals, 10th in assists and 6th in total points.

There may have been other reasons why he retired. It wasn't until five years later that Primeau found out he was a diabetic, and now he wonders if the lack of energy he felt near the end of his playing career might have been increased by that.

When he finally retired for good, Primeau went to work for Woodmansee Foods as a salesman. After that company went out of business two years later, he started working for the LaCross Company out of Toledo. Though it changed names many times because of mergers and buyouts, Primeau stayed with the company until he retired in 1996, finally leaving as a vice president.

He was done working, but diabetes kept giving Primeau complications. In the fall of 1998 he was told he needed a kidney transplant. Primeau and Sonja and their children went to the University of Michigan hospital to try and find a donor match. Randy Potts, husband of Primeau's daughter, Pam, also was tested. Two weeks later the tests came back, and everyone was shocked that Potts was a near-perfect match.

``We couldn't believe it," Primeau said. ``We just thought it was kind of neat that he was going to test."

The successful transplant was made September 30, though Primeau suffered a minor heart attack two days later. He was soon back up and running full speed.

``I'm just glad I could help," Potts said. ``They are the greatest people. They absolutely would do anything for you, and that's why I didn't think twice about doing it."

Potts had to use up his vacation for two years and missed some income, but the Komets Oldtimers stepped up by selling raffle books to help out. The idea came when Len Thornson, Ken Ullyot, Bob Chase and Gerry Randall were playing golf one day.

``We try to stick together," Randall said. ``When someone gets in trouble, we help each other because you never know when it's your turn. If you had to name a top five of the players who ever played here Reggie would be one of them, and he's a terrific person. He and Sonja are probably the greatest parents and grandparents in Fort Wayne."

There were plenty of fans and former Komets such as Ron Leef and Bill McNaught who wanted to help out. The former Komets truly are a tight fraternity.

``It's really something to see people get involved for a guy like Reggie," Randall said. ``No one wants something like this to happen to anybody, but all the ups and downs we had in hockey taught us a lot when taking on something as serious as this. We seem to have an edge on people. We just seem to know how to rise to that level to get things done."

Primeau, who had previously taken part in similar raffles for others, said he wasn't surprised. Isn't that what teammates are for?

"It's not the money, but the thought they are there to help," said Primeau. "It was just nice to hear all these guys were getting behind it. It was a very positive thing for me.

``The great thing about being a Komet was that we played together, but we also took turns having parties on the weekends after the games," Primeau said. ``We'd just sit around and have a good time. We were real close and we still are."

Other than boosting his spirits, Primeau's teammates could not do much to help him with his next health battle. In October 2000, doctors were forced to amputate Primeau's right leg below the knee because of complications from diabetes. They tried stopping the gangrene by first taking his big toe and then his remaining toes before finally giving up and taking the leg.

Primeau fought his way out of the wheelchair, walking by Christmas of that year with a prosthetic leg. On New Year's Day, after a family gathering, he tried skating on it for the first time.

"He was real excited to show everybody," said his grandson, Ryan Potts, who played at Northland College in Ashland, Mich. "A guy like him doesn't want to let anybody down, but I could tell he wasn't going to be able to do it when he put his skates on and started walking."

Because he loves to golf, Primeau's prosthesis has an ankle joint, which is not conducive to skating because of a lack of ankle support. Primeau took one step onto the Memorial Coliseum ice that day and crashed when his leg couldn't hold up. Primeau could only hold onto the boards and pull himself along for short distances.

"I just went up to him and said something to try to make him feel better," Potts said. "I said, `Grandpa, you never would have imagined that you would have had this opportunity right now when you were lying in that hospital bed for a month. Look at the positives.' "

Primeau kept his chin up and made a list of goals. First, he wanted to be able to walk without a limp so no one could tell he was wearing a prosthetic. Then he wanted to swim, "but the only problem was I swam in circles," he said with a chuckle. He also wanted to play golf again. His swing isn't perfect now, but it's respectable.

But his ultimate goal was to skate again, to recapture the sound and the feeling he missed so much. He'd often go to McMillen Park Ice Arena to watch his grandkids skate or play.

"We would have discussions, just the two of us sometimes," said McMillen manager Mitzi Toepfer. "I could just tell by the look in his eye when he watched those kids skating by how much he really, really missed it. He'd just shake his head and go, 'I don't think I'll ever be able to skate again,' and I kept saying, 'No, we'll figure out something.'"

The something turned out to be Kent Turnbow of SRT Prosthetics and Orthotics, who himself lost his right leg in a car accident as a teenager. He had regained his skating ability, but the one hitch was that Turnbow's prosthetic didn't have an ankle joint, making skating much easier.

"We had to adjust (Reggie's) skate so it would stay in alignment," Turnbow said. "The skate wanted to turn in so we brought him out to the office several times to try different things. Eventually we took an ankle brace and put it inside the skate, which stiffened up the joint."

Primeau started by walking the SRT hallways wearing his skates, and a week later he was at McMillen to try them on the ice. When he finally strode onto the ice, Primeau had stiff legs but started to slowly glide by simply moving his legs. For the first time in eight years he was truly skating.

"At least it looked like I was really skating," Primeau said. "I didn't think I would be able to get my right leg off the ice, but it came."

"He started out not picking his skates up, and then I realized he was skating faster than I was without doing that," Turnbow said with a laugh. "It probably took 15 minutes before he was able to start picking his feet up a little bit."

Within 30 minutes, Primeau was making turns and skating figure-eights.

"He was so excited it brought tears to my eyes, but I didn't want him to see me all blubbery," Toepfer said. "It was just so wonderful to see the look on his face."

Primeau shed a few tears of his own when he reached the other end of the rink, where no one could see.

"I was really happy," he said. "I didn't do any real fast skating, just so I could get my legs moving. I think it's going to work out OK. I think I'm going to be able to move pretty good."

He skated for an hour and 20 minutes, and even after going more than 100 times around the rink he didn't want to come off. When he finished, Primeau and Toepfer walked down to the other end where the Komets were starting practice to talk to Coach Greg Puhalski and the players.

"Whatever he wants to do, he'll do," Ryan Potts said. "I would love to be able to skate with him and pass it around one more time. I never thought I'd be able to get that chance, but that would be so cool. I'm sure he could still teach me a few pointers."

Today Primeau continues to play golf. He and Sonja have stayed in Fort Wayne to watch their grandsons play hockey, and simply because Fort Wayne is now home.

``We had been to so many places and traveled so much that when we came to Fort Wayne we were hoping this was it," Sonja said. ``The only thing we missed about Canada was our families. We missed a lot there, but we tried to go home every year."

Fort Wayne became further cemented as their home on October 26, 2001 when Primeau's No. 12 was lifted to the Memorial Coliseum rafters.

Reggie Primeau's careers statistics Playing Regular season *Playoffs

Season	Team	League	GP	G	A	PTS	PIM	GP	G	A	PTS	PIM
58-59	Troy	IHL	29	5	14	19	18	*	*	*	*	*
58-59	Trois Rivieres	QHL	7	1	0	1	2	*	*	*	*	*
59-60	Greensboro	EHL	7	0	3	3	12	*	*	*	*	*
59-60	Milwaukee	IHL	57	39	51	90	22	*	*	*	*	*
60-61	Portland	WHL	28	3	7	10	2	*	*	*	*	*
60-61	Fort Wayne	IHL	27	7	18	25	5	8	6	5	11	9
61-62	Fort Wayne	IHL	67	39	66	105	40	*	*	*	*	*
62-63	Fort Wayne	IHL	70	36	48	84	19	11	5	8	13	6
63-64	Fort Wayne	IHL	70	27	56	83	30	12	3	6	9	4
64-65	Fort Wayne	IHL	64	34	50	84	14	10	3	8	11	2
65-66	Fort Wayne	IHL	27	16	15	31	6	6	1	1	2	7
67-68	Fort Wayne	IHL	72	23	57	80	21	6	2	3	5	0
68-69	Fort Wayne	IHL	55	18	32	50	8	6	2	0	2	4

TERRY PEMBROKE

CHAPTER 9

In 1978 during Terry Pembroke's last season before retiring, Komets forward Dan Bonar was called up to play in the American Hockey League. Before Bonar left, Pembroke told him, ``Twenty years ago they sent me down for two weeks. Could you tell them I'm ready now?"

Terry Pembroke didn't actually play 20 years for the Komets, but at times it seemed like he was always on the Fort Wayne blue line, and because of his physical style many times he probably felt like he had played for 20 years. No one played more games for the Komets, 864 from 1964 to 1978 with a couple of seasons in the Central Hockey League thrown in.

When he finally did retire, the Komets honored Pembroke by lifting his No. 5 number to the Memorial Coliseum rafters on January 30, 1982.

In fact, Pembroke had been a Komet for so long he was the player who would put a 5 year-old named Colin Chin onto the ice to skate between periods in 1965. Exactly 30 years later, Chin finished up 10 years with the Komets in 1995-96. One of Pembroke's favorite memories is pictured on his website, cowboytexas.com, showing him waving his cowboy hat at center ice next to Chin on opening night of that season.

``For some reason I had never had a chance to talk to him before I showed up that night," Pembroke said. ``He looked at me and goes `How cool is this?' "

Almost as cool as Pembroke's life has been. As he says, ``I'm 63 and I've never had a job. How great is that?"

In many ways, Pembroke has led a charmed life, but often he fought it every step of the way, and his hockey career almost never got started.

Terry Pembroke was born April 22, 1944, in Toronto, the son of Terry Sr., and Etta Mae. She was a horsewoman first and then a teacher for 46 years, including 40 in a one-room schoolhouse. His father was a superior athlete who reached Class AAA as a centerfielder in the Boston Braves organization before he was shot in the shoulder during World War II in Italy. He then became a pitcher and later a Golden Gloves champion and a club fighter.

``I had to live up to his athletic reputation and his name," Pembroke said. ``The problem was he was one of those guys who everybody loved. He was just perfect. The only sport he never played was hockey. That's why I chose hockey."

Ironically, Pembroke sort of had hockey chosen for him. After his family moved to Meaford, Ontario when he was five, he continued skating but he didn't start playing hockey until he was 10 and he quickly jumped through several age levels. He also got into all kinds of trouble away from the rink.

When he was 12, Pembroke got into a fight on a circus midway and was busted for drinking.

``I got into a hassle with a guy on the midway and I thought I was pretty tough so they invited me back after the show," he said. ``They had 10 circus toughs and my friends all left me. I stayed there and took a pretty good thumping."

To add insult to his many injuries, he also got arrested for disorderly conduct.

The chief of police came to the Pembroke household to talk about reform school, causing his mother to cry.

``It finally dawned on me that I could be in some trouble."

He never considered that his parents might actually be conspiring with the police chief to get him some guidance.

In court Pembroke pleaded guilty to all the charges, and the judge started explaining the mandatory sentencing guidelines. By this time, Pembroke was shaking.

``Right at the end, he says, `Or....' and the police chief stood up and said, `Your honor, this kid thinks he's a hockey player. Let's let him prove it,' " Pembroke said.

The chief, Tom Sims, just happened to be the coach of the local midget hockey team, and the judge put Pembroke on probation into the chief's custody. He had to report to the chief every night and play for his team. The compromise worked out well for everyone.

When he was 13, Pembroke was drafted by the Toronto Maple Leafs, except it wasn't an official draft because he was too young. At 14 he was allowed to play for a local senior team, which was unprecedented.

``I went up for the playoffs, and that's where I learned the hipcheck from an old pro named Harry Kazarian," Pembroke said. ``He was master of it. He could just kill people with it, and he worked with me."

Though Kazarian was only about 5-5 and 200 pounds, Pembroke said, he was a mechanic of hip checks and taught how to set up opponents for them.

During Pembroke's first game, the opponents' tough guy was charging down the ice when Pembroke caught him with a hip check.

``He must have gone 20 feet in the air," Pembroke said. ``That was all the fans and the press would talk about. We went back to play them the night after that in their building. On the first shift I'm behind the net after I passed the puck when I hear my teammates screaming. I look up to see this guy coming at me with his stick headed for my throat. It was all I could do to get my hand up and I broke my wrist."

Two weeks later he played in a midget tournament wearing a cast and hitting everyone. The Maple Leafs tried to sign him for real this time, as did the Red Wings, but Pembroke liked the New York Rangers executive Emile Francis and Lyn Patrick so he signed with them. The Rangers sent him to Guelph for a couple of years where he got to play with such future NHL greats as Rod Gilbert and Jean Ratelle during their last seasons in junior. When they left, he was the only 20 year old on a team full of 16 year olds. He complained so much that

Francis allowed Pembroke to turn pro and sent him to Baltimore in the American Hockey League.

``So the last game I played in Kitchener was New Year's Day and it was against the Red Wings," Pembroke said. ``They had a guy named Campbell that I owed. I hunted him the entire game and I finally got him in the corner and jacked him up off his feet onto the glass, but when he fell, he fell down on me. Right between the skate and the shinpad there's a 1/4-inch spot that was bare and not protected, and that's where his skate blade came down and sliced all the tendons in my foot."

Supposedly, that was the end of Pembroke's hockey career. The team doctors wanted to just sew the tendons back together, but that meant Pembroke would have to walk with essentially a club foot. Pembroke protested that he wasn't going to get the surgery done until he had more input.

While this was going on, a nurse brought an orderly in to see Pembroke. The man was a doctor who had emigrated from Hungary during the Communist takeover but because he lacked the proper qualifications, he was not allowed to work as a doctor in Canada. The man told Pembroke that he knew of a surgery that could help him. As the man explained it, it was similar to the Chinese Fingers trick but for tendons. The Rangers pulled enough strings with the government that the man was allowed to perform the surgery. Pembroke figured he had nothing to lose.

After being in complete traction for seven weeks after the surgery, Pembroke was allowed to ride horses as part of his rehabilitation. The rehab worked to a point. Pembroke was able to play again, but he never had the same mobility. He also switched from left to right defense.

``I could never turn correctly going backwards because of that," he said. ``I couldn't turn into the boards."

When he tried to make that step during NHL training camps, the speedy wingers could exploit the weakness coming down the left side.

The Rangers sent Pembroke to the New York Rovers, their Eastern Hockey League affiliate. The EHL was brutally tough, and the rookie earned 60 penalty minutes in only 13 games. Pembroke compared the league to the one in ``Slapshot.'' In particular he remembers playing in New York one night and then riding the bus all the way to Jacksonville, Florida for a game the next night. Despite the caliber of play and the travel, there were other benefits.

``It was fun being in the city because nobody knew the difference between the Rangers and the Rovers, and I told everybody I was a Ranger,'' he said.

But it wasn't too long before Pembroke begged Francis to get him out of the league. He and disgruntled Rangers forward Dick Duff went out drinking for three days. Duff finally read in the paper that he had been traded to Montreal (where he won four Stanley Cups in five years). Pembroke called Francis who told him he was headed to...

``I got the 'Fort' part of it, and at that time Detroit's had a Central Hockey League team in Fort Worth,'' Pembroke said. ``He said I had to be on the plane tomorrow.''

So Pembroke got on the plane. When it arrived, he got off the plane and there was a December blizzard going on, and Pembroke said to himself, ``How in the hell can it snow this much in Texas?'' Then he met Komets coach Eddie Long who was there to pick him up, wearing his buzz cut as usual.

``I had long hair and I was carrying my guitar and I didn't have my skates,'' Pembroke said, laughing. ``He didn't think too much of me, and I'll never forget that haircut.''

It turned out Francis and Komets General Manager Ken Ullyot were very good friends, and that's how the deal was arranged. After hearing Pembroke could be an attitude problem, Ullyot arranged for him to live in a boarding house with a little old lady. After living in Manhattan, Pembroke only lasted about a week there before moving in with Cal Purinton and developing a life-long friendship.

``They were pretty darn good together on and off the ice," broadcaster Bob Chase said. "Cal was the rusher and Terry stayed at home. Cal could handle anybody, but in those days you could end up with two or three guys piling on top, and Pembroke was always there to watch out for Cal."

The relationship between Ullyot and Pembroke took a little more time, but eventually each man developed tremendous respect for the other.

``I always thought he had a big ego," Ullyot said with a laugh. ``He had a great opinion of himself, and maybe he thought I did too, but I could overcome his."

Toward the end of the 1964-65 season, Purinton, Pembroke and Bill Orban provided some toughness the Komets had been lacking, especially against Des Moines, which had Ivan Prediger, John Bailey, Joe Kiss and Pat Ginnell. The Komets beat the Oak Leafs that spring in the Turner Cup Finals to win their second championship.

``We had some knock down drag outs with Des Moines," Pembroke said. ``They turned the lights off in the coliseum to stop the fighting one night. Patty Ginnell and I started the brawl and then Purinton and Joe Kiss and then Cy Whiteside. They had a couple of guys who were just animals. So Ginnell and I are fighting and then everybody got into it and they turned the lights off. Ginnell says, `Don't you swing, you SOB, I can't see.' I said, `It works both ways.' By the time the lights came back on we were laughing."

Pembroke played three years with the Komets, mainly sticking to the defensive end or the penalty box. Away from the ice, he got involved with a bar called Club Angel off Decatur Road.

He had a deal with Francis that he could stay in Fort Wayne, but then Francis got reassigned in the Rangers' organization, and the new head man sent Pembroke to Omaha of the CHL, though the defenseman tried fighting the assignment. Hoping to throw a monkey wrench into those plans, Pembroke said the Rangers had to take Purinton, too.

They fully expected to turn around and go back to Fort Wayne. Purinton came back after one season, but Pembroke got stuck for two, including several call-ups to Buffalo of the AHL. Whenever the Bisons were about to play Hershey, which had several tough guys, Pembroke would be called up. He'd go out for warm-ups and only be told after that if he was playing depending on who dressed for Hershey. He said he went through warm-ups many times to play in three games.

After those two years in Omaha, Phoenix of the World Hockey Association wanted to sign Pembroke, but he decided to come back to Fort Wayne, in part because he had several outside business interests going, including training horses, which Pembroke loved every bit as much as hockey. He comes from five generations of farmers and ranchers.

His paternal grandfather Colonel Harry E. Pembroke had fought in two world wars on horseback, and his maternal grandfather and his mother also passed their love of horses onto Terry.

``I never made a big deal out of it because in my New York contract and then in my Fort Wayne contract I could not snow ski or rodeo," he said. ``They didn't want me getting hurt."

Which of course leads to another story.

``One year (1975-76) the kid I was playing defense with was Marc Gaudreault," Pembroke said. ``I remember taking the team out to my little ranch out there on the north side. We partied and rode horses for the better part of a weekend and he got hurt. He had to stay crippled until he got to the arena so he could go out and fall on the ice so the organization did not know we were riding horses. That was the last time I had a riding party during the season."

At one time Pembroke, along with assistant Janet Madden, had about 20 horses he was working with. He'd buy unbroken horses from Shipshewana and then ride them and sell them.

Besides the 1965 Turner Cup, Pembroke got to play on two great Komets teams. In 1972-73 he and Purinton were part of another Turner Cup championship under coach Marc Boileau. Pembroke, Purinton and Robbie Irons provided the centerpieces of a transition between two eras of Komets hockey.

``Boileau was the consummate pro who knew how to handle people,'' Pembroke said. ``If there's such a thing as a generic championship, it might have been that one because it was just a true team effort. It was just everybody busted their butts and there were some talented kids on that team. It was just a bunch of guys playing hard.''

That squad was coasting along in second place with a 31-19-2 record when they caught fire with 22 games left. By going 17-4-1 the rest of the way, the Komets ran down Dayton for the Huber Trophy and then blitzed through the two rounds of the playoffs in only nine games, beating Port Huron in the finals after losing to the Wings in the playoffs the year before. Pembroke had his best season statistically, scoring career highs with 10 goals and 57 points in 74 games.

"Those stats were due only because of a very talented partner," Pembroke said.

The other memorable team for Pembroke came in 1977-78 when Greg Pilling arrived in Fort Wayne to coach the Komets. The only problem was Pembroke had decided to retire after the previous season. The two had been teammates in Omaha, and Pilling convinced Pembroke to come back for one more season.

``The biggest thing that made Pilling great was he knew what it took to be a coach in that day and age,'' Pembroke said. ``All that Vince Lombardi stuff was dead in the water. The reason he was so successful was he was more of a psychologist and he was willing to let the personalities shine in order to get to the end goal.''

After finishing 32-36-10 in 1976-77 under Ralph Keller, the Komets came back under Pilling to go 40-23-17 and win the Huber Trophy. Pembroke played 61 games, scoring 17 points and earning 33 penalty minutes.

``The first and probably only speech Pilling ever made that year, he walked into the dressing room, and he's looking down at all these kids, and he goes `Listen. Let's get something straight. This is not the NHL, this is the IHL, you're not going to get rich, and we're here to play hockey because you either love it or you can't get a job back home. We're never getting wealthy or going to the show so let's try and have a little fun and try and maintain our dignity.' That's how he ran the entire year. We were not the most talented team, but he got lots out of miles out of journeymen kind of players. People plopped down money to see what was going to happen next."

Though he always said playing hockey beats having a real job and delays having to grow up, Pembroke finally retired, and this time no one had the chance to talk him out of it. Luckily, he played through the final season in relatively good health, and he had already set up plans to work with world champion horse trainer Keith Barnett who had moved to Indiana. So after the Komets' final playoff loss to Toledo, he drank a six pack, took his skates off and threw them over the Columbia Street bridge and by 8 a.m. the next morning he was riding horses in Logansport.

``Pemmer was a great teammate," center Terry McDougal said. ``I played with him for about three years at the end of his career. He was a more stay-at-home defenseman those years, and was definitely a great shotblocker. He was fearless at throwing his body in front of shots, and I always remember him having one sore body part or another from doing it. I so admired that about him because it was something I never had the nerve to do."

Pembroke finished with 864 games, 66 goals and 273 assists for 339 points, and he also earned 1,143 penalty minutes. When he retired, Pembroke was second to Purinton on the Komets' all-time penalty minute list, and now he's seventh. He's also third all-time in scoring by a defenseman behind Jim Burton and Lionel Repka, which is amazing considering he had only one season with more than 40 points during his career. He's also third in career playoff games with 80 behind Len Thornson and Chin, and appeared in a club-record eight all-star games, scoring a goal and four points.

More than his statistics, Pembroke became known for his hip checks. He rarely used them early in games, or more than once. All he wanted to do was get the opponents wondering when it would be coming, especially the opponents' top forwards. Saginaw's Dennis Desrosiers was a particularly favorite target.

``Desrosiers was the epitome of tough, and I liked him," Pembroke said. "I never hit him in Fort Wayne, but I would wait until we got to Saginaw and he would get irate. I would spend the better part of a two-game series setting him up for one, and he was always looking for it. Big guys are the ones you want to go after because they can't get up.

``You play a game with the forward and give him an opening he thinks he can get through and then you close it up. It makes for a hell of a crash. The biggest thing is you make them think they beat you. Once you do it to them, you've got them thinking about it all the time. It did more for the crowd than it hurt anybody."

Opposing skaters weren't the only ones in the arena with an eye out for a Pembroke hip check.

``That's a lost art today," McDougall said. ``it's all about being a great backward skater and pinpoint timing. He was incredible at it. The crowd absolutely loved it."

As Chase said, "He took people up the wall and they didn't get up. Oh, God, could he hit."

He could also fight, though he never racked up huge penalty minute numbers.

"He was good enough that he didn't have to do it too often," Chase said. "I can't ever remember seeing him get beat up. He used to fight with a smile on his face, and that used to really scare people."

Primarily a defensive defenseman who spent more time on the penalty kill than the power play, Pembroke's numbers were never as flashy or as hard-hitting as his hip checks. He had a reputation for never coughing the puck up in his own end no matter how hard a licking he took. He was also a leader by example who wasn't afraid to say something if he thought it needed said. Because he rarely said anything, when he did everyone paid attention.

Though he didn't score often, Pembroke was still a threat from virtually anywhere on the ice as he showed on February 20, 1965. With about 25 seconds left in the first period against Toledo, Pembroke scored one of the most remarkable goals in Komets' history. After recovering a loose puck off a face-off, Pembroke started to skate behind the Komets' net and out of trouble when the Toledo forwards stopped chasing him, figuring the period was almost over. Pembroke then turned, figured what the heck and lifted a wrist shot from the bottom edge of the face-off circle.

Usually when Pembroke tried it, the shot would land and skip toward the goaltender but not this time. After traveling 176 feet through the air and passing by the Memorial Coliseum scoreboard, the puck hit goaltender Glenn Ramsay in the leg and amazingly bounced into the goal. Reports at the time said the puck skipped in front of Ramsay, but the goaltender later told Pembroke at an IHL All-Star Game that he lost the puck in the crowd of 8,013 fans and was waiting for it to hit the ice so he could react.

``He said he just never thought anybody would shoot that high,'' Pembroke said. ``The fact that it was Ramsay made it twice as funny because he was so good.''

Ramsay, a former Komet, was perhaps the greatest IHL goaltender of all time.

``I'm glad I was able to help Terry be remembered,'' a good-natured Ramsay said in 1997. ``I'm glad somebody profited from it.''

Pembroke was just as competitive away from the rink, even in retirement. Because of his age and background, he got a late start, but within 10 years he was a National Cutting Horse Association futurity finalist. He also became a nationally known trainer for cutting horses. Instead of physically touching the horses, Pembroke uses hand signals and body language to direct the horse where he wants it to go.

``This horse and I have an agreement,'' Pembroke said once, standing empty-handed at the center of the ring. ``Am I magic? No. Do I understand this animal? Yes. That's horse training in a nutshell.''

But conventional horse wisdom says he shouldn't be able to do it his way. Tradition says horses can't be trained unless someone is perched on their backs. As a result of his success, Pembroke has become a controversial figure in horse training, especially regarding the horses he works with the most, Arabians. He was quoted in a horse magazine as saying Arabians are good only for ``beauty contests," and coming out of a competition he once compared it to ``walking into a $10 million pet store."

Not surprisingly, in the horse industry he's seen as something of an eccentric. He's not sure if Arabian owners are upset with him because they feel he's showing the horses no respect, or if they just don't like his style. Pembroke figures he's giving the animals plenty of respect by providing them with possibilities after their show careers are over.

``I always loved the breed, but their owners are a real high-brow, egotistical group of people," Pembroke said. ``I think half of it is that somebody actually came in and did what they always said couldn't be done. The point is these horses are good for lots of things, but they've never been allowed to do them. The bottom line is that I'm right, and I know what I'm talking about."

Against conventional wisdom, Pembroke developed a system that essentially uses cows to train stock horses at liberty, taking advantage of the horse's natural traits. His system convinces the horse to want to do the work rather than fight it.

Pembroke never gets onto a horse during the initial training. He teaches them from the center of a ring. He believes the younger a horse can be taught, the more options its owner has if the horse isn't good enough for shows.

``A lot of times even when people see it, they think it's a circus trick," he said. ``The horsemen understand it, but the people who `think' they are horsemen, they see it and they think that because I do it in a round pen I have invisible cues. Then I do it with their horses, and then they think, well maybe it's the horses."

The other radical theory he has is that Pembroke treats the horses like athletes and not as cattle. He also takes pride in working with horses everyone else has given up on. He gives them a new purpose.

``I spend a tremendous amount of time on conditioning and training," he said. ``The stock horse depends so much on genetics. What they miss is you can take that superstar and get him in shape the same as a hockey player or a football player. It's the same thing with the horses. I'm not doing anything mind boggling here; I'm just helping them build every muscle that they use so thy can be better than the competition."

Pembroke now lives in LaGrange, Texas, training horses and sometimes coming back to Fort Wayne to give exhibitions and visit friends. He's starting to dream of competing again if he can find the right horse to go after a world title.

Loyalty is one of Pembroke's trademarks as much as his cowboy hat. If one of his friends needs him, Pembroke will be there as soon as possible. And he's loyal to Fort Wayne.

"He's a very genuine guy, and a lot of people misunderstood him because he does have a swagger, but that's just Terry," Chase said. "I just feel honored to think whenever Terry comes to town I get a phone call or he stops by. I didn't always like him, especially early in his career. I thought he was a little too swaggery, but when you got to know Terry, you found out he wasn't a phony at all."

About the only time Pembroke got truly upset with folks in Fort Wayne was in the late 1980s when David Welker owned the team. Welker thought it would be OK to hand out some of the retired numbers to active players. Pembroke wasn't so much upset for himself as he was for the other retired legends.

``The reason Fort Wayne was and is successful is because they operate with big league scruples," he said. ``The thing that kept that hockey team going was the links to the past. Every generation draws a certain group of people, and then eventually they all show up at the arena. Everybody in Fort Wayne knows a Komet, either a current one or a former Komet. It's just a unique municipality."

Pembroke said he rarely mentions his hockey career while he's working in his horse career, but every once in a while someone will recognize him and ask about it. Sometimes it happens in the oddest place.

``There was this one lady in Seattle, Washington, who came up to me after a show," he said. "She and her husband had gone out there in the aerospace program, and the next night I bet she had 30 people out there to talk to me."

Even when he was playing in other cities, Pembroke said Fort Wayne was still home, and he says part of him has never left. He still talks to at least two or three people from Fort Wayne every day.

``If it didn't snow in Fort Wayne, I would never have left there," he said. ``I will never, ever drop my ties there."

Not even if the NHL finally calls back.

Terry Pembroke's careers statistics Playing Regular season*Playoffs

Season	League	Team	GP	G	A	PTS	PIM	GP	G	A	PTS	PIM
64-65	EHL	New York	13	0	3	3	60	*	*	*	*	*
64-65	IHL	Fort Wayne	56	7	11	18	99	9	0	3	3	16
65-66	IHL	Fort Wayne	70	2	15	17	143	6	1	1	2	18
66-67	IHL	Fort Wayne	72	4	17	21	142	13	0	2	2	34
67-68	CHL	Omaha	70	2	17	19	83	*	*	*	*	*
68-69	CHL	Omaha	57	6	12	18	71	2	0	0	0	9
68-69	AHL	Buffalo	3	0	0	0	2	*	*	*	*	*
69-70	IHL	Fort Wayne	68	5	34	39	163	3	1	0	1	2
70-71	IHL	Fort Wayne	66	2	16	18	72	5	0	2	2	8
71-72	IHL	Fort Wayne	72	7	28	35	130	8	2	3	5	14
72-73	IHL	Fort Wayne	74	10	47	57	133	9	0	1	1	10
73-74	IHL	Fort Wayne	34	3	9	12	36	*	*	*	*	*
74-74	IHL	Fort Wayne	73	4	24	28	10	*	*	*	*	*
75-76	IHL	Fort Wayne	71	8	15	23	59	9	1	5	6	2
76-77	IHL	Fort Wayne	67	4	23	27	42	9	1	2	3	2
77-78	IHL	Fort Wayne	61	3	14	17	33	9	1	1	2	14

ROBBIE IRON

CHAPTER 10

Like any boy growing up in Canada, Robbie Irons always dreamed of playing in the National Hockey League, becoming a regular and then an all-star before maybe leading his team to the Stanley Cup. As the fate of his hockey career kept twisting, Irons was successful but always seemed to miss by inches in his reach for his ultimate goals.

Showing all the inner calm necessary to be a top-flight goaltender, Irons never became too frustrated, and eventually realized his life has been pretty special because he's been able to fulfill his more-important personal goals.

``To live the life that I did, it was a dream," he said. ``If I had a chance to do it over again, I'd go back and do it again."

Robbie Richard Irons was born November 11, 1946 in Toronto to Bob, a postman, and his wife Vie who worked for the government in the baby bonus department. Robbie learned to skate when he was five on the small backyard rink his father built each winter. They used potato sacks from his grandfather's grocery store to build a goal net. The neighbors also built a rink, but there was a fence between the yards – until about halfway through the season. Each spring the fathers rebuilt the fence. By then the boys were playing a different form of hockey.

``We used to play street hockey all the time and a friend of mine got a goalie glove from somewhere," Irons said. ``I could catch with it and I liked it."

When he was six years old, Irons' father took him to Keelesdale Park where he joined his first organized team and received his first goalie pads. His father would get hand-me-down skates from people off his postal route until Robbie received his own first pair as a Christmas gift at age nine. After Irons outgrew his first pads at age 12 or 13, he started wearing an old pair his uncle had used while playing in Scotland for the Canadian Armed Forces where one of his teammates was original Komet George Drysdale.

Irons was successful very early, leading his Keelesdale team to a Pee Wee championship which led to more opportunities with a sponsored team. The next year Irons' team won a city championship.

At age 15, Irons joined a Hamilton junior team that was sponsored by the Detroit Red Wings. The Red Wings wanted to send Irons to Flin Flon, but he decided to stay in Toronto. Playing for a poor team meant he was often bombarded but the team folded after the season, leaving Irons with a decision to make. The Etobicoke Indians of the same league needed a goaltender, but their regular goaltender was Ken Dryden.

``My dad was against it but I felt I was going to be getting some hockey and Dryden was only going to be there a year before he went away to college," Irons said. ``I didn't play a lot, maybe 10 games that year, but I subsidized it by playing for a senior team with my uncle."

Irons' gamble worked, and the next year he led Etobicoke to the junior B championship as the MVP of the playoffs. That led to signing the next year to play in Junior A with Kitchener where the team had the league's best goals against average. Irons' career continued to climb. That summer he talked to the New York Rangers who wanted to send him to their Central Hockey League team in Omaha. A contract would be discussed at training camp.

But while playing baseball that summer, Irons was hit by a pitch on the left arm, hard enough that the ball rolled down the third baseline long enough that the umpire thought it had hit his bat. Irons walked on the next pitch but didn't realize the injury's extent until he tried breaking up a play at second base. After rolling over on the broken arm, Irons threw up. Within two hours, he was in surgery.

One great thing about that summer was Irons became engaged to Marilyn Coles, who drove him to the hospital after the game. By the time he moved to Kitchener in the fall of 1966, Irons had graduated from high school so he worked in a print shop. Marilyn was a receptionist at Kauffman Rubber, a winter footwear factory, and they met while riding the bus to work. They were married September 6, 1968.

When it came time for training camp, Irons was still recovering and the Rangers sent him home, saying they'd find him a spot when he was ready. That December, the Rangers sent him to Fort Wayne, where Ken Ullyot had strong ties with New York.

In a preview of things to come, Irons had a shutout in his first game at Memorial Coliseum against Des Moines. Irons played 43 games that season, splitting time with veteran Gerry Randall, and wearing jersey No. 1, not No. 30 as he would later.

Then Irons caught a good break. On June 13, 1968, the Rangers traded Irons and Camille Henry to the expansion St. Louis Blues for Bill Plager, Don Caley and Wayne Rivers. Blues coach Scotty Bowman was building a goaltending tandem of future Hall of Famers Jacques Plante, 39, and Glenn Hall, 37.

``I met Scotty Bowman in downtown Toronto and he told me he wanted to sign three young goaltenders to back up Glenn Hall and Jacques Plante," Irons said. ``I was all for it. Scotty was always thinking outside the box. He knew he had two older guys and he needed to cut down on the travel time or it was going to wear them out."

Bowman signed Irons, Gary Edwards and Ted Oimet, sending two of them to play with the Blues' farm team in Kansas City while the other would serve as a practice goalie and back up either Plante or Hall during road games. If the Blues had a weekend road trip to Minnesota and Chicago, Plante or Hall would go straight to Chicago to wait for the team while Irons backed up the other in Minnesota. The season was split into thirds as the third goalies rotated with Irons starting the first third in St. Louis.

Irons, 21, practiced every day and dressed with the Blues for more than 60 games over the next three seasons, wearing either No. 1 or No. 30 depending on whom he was backing up, taking the other goaltender's number.

``You just had to bide your time," Irons said.

His time came on Nov. 13, 1968, appropriately enough in a game at New York against the Rangers. The Blues and Plante had played the night before in Boston so Hall was in net when the Rangers' Vic Hatfield ripped a long slap shot that dipped under Hall's arm and into the goal. Hall charged out to protest that Hatfield's stick had to be illegal and bumped into the referee to earn a game misconduct.

The referee skated to the St. Louis bench to tell Bowman to get his backup into the game. Bowman walked over to Irons and told him to take his time during the warm-up and then come back to the bench to see him. After a regular warm-up, which was permitted at the time, Irons came to the bench and Bowman instructed him to go with the trainer into the locker room with a supposed leg injury.

``The trainer is messing around when Scotty comes in yelling at the referee, who says, `C'mon, let's go, You gotta go,' '' Irons said. ``I don't really know what's going on other than I'm antsy and the building is jam packed. So finally, out I come and the crowd is going crazy. They finally get me in the net and we get started. I handled the puck a couple of times, and I think I might have made one save. Before I know it, three and a half minutes later I look over and who's standing on the bench dressed but Jacques Plante who had been sitting in the stands. Scotty calls me over and in Jacques Plante goes. Then they gotta give him a warmup.''

Bowman came down to the end of the bench and told Irons he did a good job. The Blues won 2-1, but the Rangers started a huge argument with the league office that led to a rule change. After that game, teams were limited to the two goaltenders listed on the lineup card.

``As a young kid, I didn't know how I would handle it, but when I went in, I was shaking in my boots, there's no doubt about it,'' Irons said. ``The fooling around upset me from the standpoint of `C'mon, let's get going, I don't need this Mickey Mouse stuff. If I'm going to play, let's go. If I'm going to fall on my face, fine. Let's get this thing going.' Once I got in there and actually handled the puck, I started to relax and feel OK. When I got out of there, I felt real good about myself. It gave me a lot of confidence and some inspiration to enjoy practice and keep doing what I was doing.''

The next year Irons played three exhibition games with St. Louis, but he never got into another NHL game. Today he holds a record with Christian Soucy and Sean Gauthier for the least minutes played in a career by an NHL goaltender with three.

He played 60 games over the next three seasons in Kansas City as Oimet and Edwards took their turns in St. Louis. Oimet played in one game with the Blues and Edwards in two during that time.

The only problem came during the third season when Bowman moved Irons back and forth to Kansas City several times which was frustrating for all three goaltenders who had no idea what Bowman was trying to do.

One day in 1970, Camille Henry was coaching Kansas City and called Irons into the office to tell him there was going to be a major shakeup the next day, but that Bowman had told him Irons would be fine. So the next day Irons was called to the phone to talk with Bowman who said, ``Robbie, I'm sorry but I don't have a job for you. Get your expenses together and see me when you come back to St. Louis.''

Upset, Irons flew to St. Louis with itemized expenses That incensed Bowman who argued over every nickel. Irons eventually got his money and also stopped in Fort Wayne. He never played in another NHL game, but the story doesn't end there. Near the end of Irons' career in 1980, he received a call one September day from Ullyot to come to the office. Ullyot had taken a call from Blues General Manager Emile Francis who wanted to talk to Irons. Ironically, Francis had been the Rangers' general manager during the 1968 game and had led the New York protest to the league.

``It jumps in my head right away that they want me to go to training camp,'' Irons said. ``He gets on the phone and says, `We've got an oldtimers game in Chicago and we need a goaltender. Glenn Hall is going to play for Chicago.' I said, `Wow, you must have looked a long ways down the list,' and he said, `Robbie, you're on the list and that's all that matters.' ''

Irons agreed to play and drove to Chicago with a buddy the next day to play on Sunday before the Komets opened training camp on Monday.

Irons walked into the dressing room and saw Bowman standing there along with some of his former teammates.

There was a full house because Bobby Hull was dressing in a Blackhawks' uniform for the first time in 10 years. Bob Johnson played in goal for St. Louis during the game's first half, and Chicago was leading 2-0 when Irons went in. He shut out Chicago the rest of the ways as the Blues ended up winning 3-2.

Chicago had the extra attacker in the final seconds, but Irons made some big saves in the final seconds. Irons has a picture of himself playing in the game wearing his Komets mask while Hull and the Blackhawks' Red Hay are battling in front of him with a St. Louis defenseman.

``So we win the game and I go into the dressing room and Scotty greeted me and said, `You're still playing? You still got a couple more years in you?' I said, `Any time.' "

During the 1994 NHL Lockout, Bowman, who was coaching the Detroit Red Wings at the time, showed up to watch a game at Memorial Coliseum. Irons was broadcasting with Bob Chase.

``I got off the radio and we talked a little bit," Irons said. ``He says, `There's never been a goaltender who knew what the hell he was talking about on radio. I"ll have to listen on the way back home.' "

Same old Scotty.

After leaving Bowman in his St. Louis office in 1970, Irons came back to Fort Wayne where Marc Boileau had just taken over as Komets coach and Jimmy Keough was in his second year manning the Fort Wayne nets. Irons was an immediate improvement, cutting a goal per game off the Komets' defensive average.

But that success didn't carry over the next season which was the toughest of Irons' career in Fort Wayne. Boileau and the Komets had developed an affiliation with the Pittsburgh Penguins which included goaltender Paul Hoganson who had a very strong season. Irons played only 21 games.

That was the last time for a decade when Irons wasn't the Komets' main man in goal. In some ways he was almost too consistent, always playing around 50 games and always giving up around 3.50 goals per game. The Komets and their fans always knew Irons could be counted on, he'd be among the best goalies in the International Hockey League and he'd be a steady presence in the locker room. He was so good, so often, he was almost taken for granted.

``It's like having that guard dog that you leave at the ranch," defenseman Terry Pembroke said. ``He was the anchor for the whole franchise. He's just solid as a player and a person. He's just there for you and that's the biggest compliment I can give."

Irons' goals against average may seem high by today's standards, but that's also partly due to the equipment which has evolved tremendously over the past 30 years. Pads were heavier, masks were harder to see out of and the goalies also had much less protection for their arms. Irons was one of the quickest goalies during his era, studied his opponents' tendencies diligently and took great pride in skating out to challenge shooters.

``The guys didn't lift the puck up high," Irons said. ``They had more control of it so I didn't get hit in the shoulder as much as I did in the feet. The other thing was that you knew who the shooters were with the six or seven teams. You knew which players were going to do what because you played them so often.

"The toughest thing was playing Friday, Saturday and Sunday, those damn horsehair pads were still wet on Sunday so the tonnage on those things was unbelievable. Water would get into them and you just didn't have enough time to dry them out. They were horsehair and leather so the tonnage on those things was unbelievable."

Almost as unbelievable was Irons' performance during the 1973 IHL All-Star Game in Dayton. With the South trailing 4-1, Irons was sent into the game, and he sparked a comeback. Almost immediately, Irons made one-on-one saves in succession against Muskegon's Gary Ford and Bob Tombari and Saginaw's Dennis Desrosiers. Irons stopped all 21 shots against him in what might be the only perfect performance by a goaltender in any all-star game ever.

``Dayton was definitely enemy territory for us, especially that season, and here they were on their edge of their seats yelling for Robbie,"

Chase said. ``On the ride home I said to Robbie, `Savor what has just happened because when we get back in there the next time you're going to be the villain.' He was an exciting goaltender, and when he was on, he was a circus to watch.''

Irons was always good to start at least half the Komets' games each season. Starting in 1972-73, for seven straight seasons and eight of the next nine, he ranked among the IHL's top 10 goaltenders, usually finishing among the top five. That's an amazing run, especially considering that the IHL of the time was known for its high-scoring games with little emphasis on defense. In fact, Irons scored 17 assists during the 1970s to easily establish the Fort Wayne franchise career record for a goaltender. It's doubtful minor league hockey will ever see that kind of offensive era again.

Despite that run and playing in five IHL All-Star Games, Irons was named a first- or second-team postseason all-star with the league only once during his career and that came after his last season in 1980-81. The Hockey News recognized his achievements in 1997 by naming Irons the IHL's second-best all-time goaltender behind Glenn Ramsay, but he never got another chance at the NHL.

``I always wondered why,'' he said. ``One of the mistakes I probably made, and my dad used to give me crap all the time about it, was the fact he thought I should have gotten an agent a long time ago. I was sort of half contented. Marilyn was happy here, I felt secure here a little bit, but that was probably the biggest mistake I made in my whole career. I never got an agent to do something for me because I always felt my ability would do it.''

One day on a plane ride back to Toronto, Irons sat next to Detroit scout Jimmy Devallano, and Irons asked what the deal was.

``Robbie, the word is you don't want to leave Fort Wayne,'' Devallano said. ``You have a house there and you don't want to leave.''

``I never said that,'' Irons said, ``I'm from the old school of believing your ability talks for you. If you think I'm good enough to play in Fort Worth or maybe even another shot at it, come scout me and see me after the game and we'll talk.''

Devallano said, ``A lot of people don't realize that.''

Irons did get one more shot, but even that seemed ill-fated. In 1974, Irons got a chance to go to training camp with the NHL expansion team the Oakland Seals who were thinking about sending Irons to their Central Hockey League farm team in Salt Lake. Irons got a letter telling him to show up in Kingston, Ontario for training camp, but when he arrived the team had just undergone a management restructuring and no one remaining knew anything about Irons. Within a few days he called Fort Wayne to re-sign with the Komets.

``There's where if I had an agent, he would have taken care of that,'' Irons said.

But he never left Fort Wayne again and became a transitional player for the Komets. When he first came to Fort Wayne, Irons played with such Komets legends as John Goodwin, Lionel Repka, Reggie Primeau, Teddy Wright and Norm Waslawski. When he came back in 1970, those players had been replaced with Cal Purinton, Ron Ullyot and Pembroke. He played with Len Thornson who was a Komets' great from the 1960s and with Dale Baldwin who was one of Fort Wayne's best players in the 1980s.

During Irons' 12 seasons, he played for six coaches, to that point more than any player in Komets history, and it's possible that no one played with a larger roster of players during his Fort Wayne career. He and Pembroke were always the players providing stability.

``He went through hell to play,'' Pembroke said. ``He just had nerves and he was so serious all the time that I used to think he would be dead by the time he was 40. He just lived and died hockey.''

For some reason, Irons had a well-known need to barf before games which started when he was a teenager. His family would eat dinner around 5:30 p.m. and he'd leave for the rink in time to arrive by 7 p.m. for an 8 p.m. game. Even when Irons ate his pre-game steak early in the afternoon as a professional, he'd still have trouble with his stomach before the game that night.

``It was just nerves," he said. ``Once I got out onto the ice, there was no problem. It was just the anticipation of getting there and the excitement, and that was the only way I could release the tension."

Several Komets team doctors suggested different remedies, but those came up as quick as anything. Getting sick became part of Irons' pre-game routine and he'd have to cut loose every night. Even his teammates noticed.

``If he wasn't chucking before the game, we didn't think he was ready," long-time teammate Robbie Laird said, laughing. ``If he was sitting there normal without going to the can, we'd be concerned. We'd be like, `C'mon, get in there and let's go so we can win this thing.' "

As soon as he got onto the ice and got going in warm-ups, Irons said his stomach would settle down and he'd be fine.

``I used to get him mad," Primeau said. ``He was real nervous so I'd get out there and just to make him relax, I had this shot where I'd shoot it and take the speed off of it like a change up. He'd give me a mean look but I did it just to get him to relax."

Strangely, Irons never had a problem with his stomach when he was coaching travel hockey or during his 12-year run with the Snider High School club team.

The pre-game illness is about as bad as things ever got for Irons, who was lucky enough to only suffer one serious injury during his career. During a game late in the 1974-75 season, Irons sustained a knee injury when he was bowled over under a forward and a defenseman.

Despite his own individual ability, Irons played on some below average Komets teams which may have contributed to his anxiety. From 1973-74 until Gregg Pilling came in 1977-78, the Komets went through four straight losing seasons, the longest such run in their history. During those seasons, Irons' goals against averages were a very strong 3.29, 3.27, 3.60 and 3.76, and he himself posted only one losing season during his entire career. This was during the era when there was usually only one or two goaltenders per year in the league with goals against averages under. 3.00.

Maybe the Komets were paying the price for winning the Turner Cup in 1972-73. They got hot late to go 17-4-1 over their last 22 games and capture the Huber Trophy as regular-season champs, and then won eight of nine games during the playoffs.

During the first playoff game against Flint, the Komets blasted the Generals 9-0, but Irons broke his thumb tangling with Generals goaltender Merlin Jenner during a last-second brawl, knocking him out for the rest of the playoffs. As rookie Don Atchison played spectacularly, it must have felt odd for Irons to be forced the watch the one time during his long career when his team advanced to the finals.

``I felt that no matter who was playing, we were going to win," Irons said. ``The gratification I got out of that, knowing I got a shutout and we had beaten that team. Even if I had been playing, I still feel we would have won. It came right down to when we played Port Huron I dressed the last game. Marc said to me with about five minutes left in the game to go in, but I said, `No, he's earned this. He's played well enough, just leave it the way it is.' "

Irons said his one real regret is that he didn't get enough pictures of the championship celebration in Port Huron.

Atchison came back the next year but struggled. It seemed like almost every season, Irons had a new goaltending partner and sometimes several in the same year as he played with 21 goaltenders during his 12 seasons with the Komets. Irons was usually a tremendous guiding influence on Komets goaltenders, particularly the younger ones and even well into his retirement.

He also convinced one potential goaltender to become a forward. Born September 25, 1974, Kevin Irons used to come to the rink as a youngster to skate after practices or try on his father's equipment in the locker room.

``One day he's in net wearing my goalie gloves with his shoes on, sliding around in the slush," Irons said. ``This is when he was about two. So we go home and he's off somewhere and we can't find him. Marilyn goes out to the garage and opens the garage door and lets out a scream. He had gone and gotten baby oil and squirted it all over the floor in the garage and then had gotten baby powder and sprinkled it all over that. He was out there playing hockey whacking the puck all over the place."

A few years later Kevin talked to his father about following in his skates to become a netminder, but Robbie discouraged his son. He suggested instead that Kevin become a forward.

``I told him, `I think you'll enjoy it a lot more, and I'll enjoy it a lot more watching you if you play somewhere else,' " Robbie said. ``I was concerned about the equipment, and I remember my dad at the games with my grandfather. They used to have to stand off to the side because they didn't want to hear the criticism from the fans and the parents and all that stuff, so I was a little leery about that. I always had the dream of playing forward, though I've never played in an organized game as a forward other than one of the Komet oldtimers games. I told him to enjoy it and from the beginning he was a goal scorer and he was a very heads up player. He knew what to do, and I was very proud of the way he handled himself."

Kevin became an accomplished player and scorer on the Snider club team. Now Kevin's son Nolan is just as inventive around games, tagging along with his father who coaches the East Noble baseball team. Kevin and his wife Chris also became parents of Carter Warren Irons in 2007.

The Irons also have a daughter, Danielle, born June 4, 1981. While Robbie and Kevin often went to hockey tournaments on the weekends, Danielle's interests turned to a different kind of performance. With Marilyn's help, Danielle started dancing at age 5. She was a cheerleader at Carroll High School and was on the dance team at Ball State, eventually becoming the squad's captain. Now she teaches Grade 2 at Perry Hill Elementary, teaches at the Northeast School of Dance and coaches the Carroll High School dance team. Just like with her brother, her proud father loves watching Danielle's teams perform.

``One of the things I see in both of them are all the ways they agonize as coaches in winning and losing and in the performing factor," he said. "I sit in the stands and I want to say something, but then I sit back. If they ask me my opinion I would give it, but they are the coaches now."

Irons continued his consistent play with the Komets through the 1980-81 season, finally pulling off his sweater for the last time after 12 seasons. Kevin was 7 years old that summer, and a daughter Danielle was 1. Irons was 35 years old when he decided to hang up his skates, the only Komet to play a full season in three different decades. He had played 573 games in the Fort Wayne net, more than twice as many as any other Komets goaltender. He also played in 50 playoff games, 17 ahead of second-place Pokey Reddick.

Irons and Pembroke had their numbers, No. 30 and No. 5, retired during ceremonies January 30, 1982. The Komets named the 5-30 Unsung Hero award named after them.

Before retiring, Irons had been working several years for Pepsi during the summers. Pepsi General Manager Ike Stang said he envisioned Irons moving into management, and gave him the responsibility of running the local version of the Pepsi Challenge and with calling on all the schools, Little Leagues and other local sporting venues. He discovered he was a natural.

``I enjoyed calling on the schools and talking to people," Irons said. ``I had a couple of high schools I'd walk into during the summer and talk to the ADs, and boom they knew me just like that. There were other machines all over the place, but I walked in and we got talking hockey and a little golf before business, and before I knew it, it was `When do you want to switch them?' "

Irons served as a key account manager for 22 years with Pepsi, then became a territorial sales manager for three years before becoming a sales support supervisor in 2007.

But Irons could not leave hockey totally behind. He started coaching Snider the year after he retired along with Robbie Laird who was sitting out a season with an injury.

``We ended up both getting suspended the first year, and I think he's still under suspension," Irons said with a laugh.

Snider had a pretty big team, a pretty good team that first season, advancing to the state tournament where the Panthers played Culver

Academy's No. 1 team. Culver led 9-0 during the second period when Snider's frustrated players started to get a little more physical with their play.

``Our kids had a lot of pride," Irons said. ``Their coach is yelling and all that so the referee comes over and says, 'Hey Coach you have to calm them down.' I said, 'You tell him to back off. He's got a 9-0 lead. He backs off and we'll finish this. He keeps piling up the score and this isn't going to be funny.' It kept getting pretty rough so with about five minutes left the ref calls the game."

So Irons and Laird were automatically suspended pending a meeting before the Indiana High School Hockey board of directors. Irons met with the board before the next season and was reinstated, but Laird returned to playing and never got his suspension lifted.

Despite usually getting frustrated with the officiating, Irons coached Snider for 12 seasons, winning three state titles and seven city championships. He was replaced by former Komet Doug Johnston who was coaching his sons.

Irons continues to hang around hockey and the Komets as Chase's color commentator for home games. He started working radio a little bit while he was with the Blues, working with Dan Kelly, and sometimes with Chase when Irons was injured during his Fort Wayne career. After Irons retired, Chase suggested he come up to the press box to help.

Like many of the Komets Oldtimers, Irons always seems to be around the games, providing memories and perspective on the franchise's long history and importance in Fort Wayne. That also provides context of what he accomplished during his long career.

``I've done a lot of things," he said. ``I had the opportunity to play Pebble Beach and go to the final four and things like that. I was at a family reunion (in 2007) in Canada, and one of them mentioned I had played professional hockey so I told a few stories. I can still sit down and talk and people are mesmerized. A lot of these former Komets never stop talking about what it was like, and it just shows how much they loved it. I guess I'm the same way. I'd do it all again."

Robbie Irons' career statistics Playing Regular season *Playoffs

Season	Team	League	GP	GA	GAA	SO	GP	GA	GAA	SO
66-67	Kitchener	OHA	32	95	2.94	3	*	*	*	*
67-68	Fort Wayne	IHL	46	134	3.35	1	4	19	0	4.35
68-69	St. Louis	NHL	1	0	0	0.00	*	*	*	*
68-69	Kansas City	CHL	24	83	0	3.80	*	*	*	*
69-70	Kansas City	CHL	30	104	2	3.47	*	*	*	*
70-71	Kansas City	CHL	6	23	0	3.83	*	*	*	*
70-71	Fort Wayne	IHL	31	80	1	2.65	4	22	0	5.50
71-72	Fort Wayne	IHL	21	83	0	4.00	*	*	*	*
72-73	Fort Wayne	IHL	46	132	2	2.89	1	0	1	0.00
73-74	Fort Wayne	IHL	47	148	2	3.29	*	*	*	*
74-75	Fort Wayne	IHL	46	148	2	3.27	*	*	*	*
75-76	Fort Wayne	IHL	63	199	1	3.60	9	49	0	5.44
76-77	Fort Wayne	IHL	41	141	1	3.76	*	*	*	*
77-78	Fort Wayne	IHL	39	129	0	3.60	7	20	0	3.76
78-79	Fort Wayne	IHL	54	193	0	3.90	13	56	0	4.29
79-80	Fort Wayne	IHL	41	147	1	4.03	14	44	1	3.28
80-81	Fort Wayne	IHL	51	168	0	3.71	11	47	0	4.45

ROBBIE LAIRD

CHAPTER 11

The worst break of Robbie Laird's career turned out to be the best break of his life.

As a 19-year-old Pittsburgh Penguins' seventh-round draft choice in 1974, Laird knew he had to make an impression in a hurry during his first NHL training camp. No one really expected much from him so he knew he had to hustle and show what he could do.

``On my very first shift on the first day, I run into Bernie Lukowich," Laird said. ``I took a run at him, and he was real solid, probably about 220 pounds, and I had my wrist in an awkward position. I ended up breaking it three places. I think I made a mistake because I played the rest of the scrimmage. I couldn't get anything done, and I don't think they were too impressed."

The Penguins told Laird to go home to Regina and they'd send him to their American Hockey League farm club in Hershey when he was healed up. About six weeks later the Penguins called to say instead they were sending him to Fort Wayne.

``At the time I had no idea where Fort Wayne was," Laird said.

Until that time he had lived his entire life in Regina. Now, in 2007, Laird has lived in Fort Wayne longer than he lived in Regina, and he can't imagine ever leaving. He jokes that he has a Komets fireball tattooed on his chest, which is only partly in jest. They can remove tattoos today, but Laird could never remove himself from the Komets.

``I consider myself a Fort Wayne Komet and always will," Laird said. ``Fort Wayne has always been great to me. From the time I came to Fort Wayne, I've been here every year. I went to play and work in other cities sometimes over the years, but home was in Fort Wayne."

Robbie Laird was born Dec. 29, 1954 to Glenn and Nona Laird in Regina, the youngest of three children. Glenn Laird worked at the Imperial Oil refinery for 25 years before taking an early retirement to follow his second dream of training thoroughbred race horses. Nona Laird worked for many years with the Royal Canadian Mounted Police.

No one knows it today, but Rob Laird was actually born Glenn Roberts Laird. His father was Glenn Edwards Laird.

``Obviously I've never used it, almost from Day 1," Rob Laird said. ``There were two Glenns in the household, and for whatever reason it was Rob or Robbie for as long as I can remember."

Like many Canadian boys, Robbie learned to skate and play hockey on a backyard rink, this one built by his grandfather. He never missed a day and later moved up to the neighborhood rinks. He started skating at age five, tumbling around for two or three years before a school program taught him the proper way to use the blades.

Laird worked his way through the youth ranks until he was lucky enough to be selected by the Regina Pats in the junior draft. Though he was listed at 5-8 or 5-9, 180 pounds, it's doubtful Laird met his measurements, but he always played bigger. Larger opponents didn't want to mess with him much because of his aggressiveness and persistence.

``My size didn't affect me a great deal growing up," he said. ``I never really thought about it. I think the way I played, I just loved the game. I played with passion, and that's where the style of play grew from."

He was scrappy, determined and he never quit. As a Komet, he developed the reputation for scoring big goals late in games to pull the team even or put it ahead. As former Komets owner, coach and general manager Ken Ullyot said, ``He always gave you everything he had."

While playing for the Pats, Laird gradually earned more ice time until his final year when he scored 39 goals and 84 points in 68 games. Pats worked their way through the playoffs to earn the Memorial Cup, boosting Laird's draft prospects.

The next year he ended up in Fort Wayne.

News-Sentinel sports editor Bud Gallmeier once wrote of Laird, ``The first time I saw Robbie Laird in a Komets uniform, I wasn't impressed. He wasn't a very good skater, and his shot never made goalies cringe. There was one thing I noticed, however, you'd usually find Laird where the puck was, especially when it was in the corners, and his stats did not vary at home or away. In anything, Laird was a better road player than he was at home... At 5 feet 8 and 180 pounds, Laird was challenged more as a rookie than most rookies are. The first time around, that is. It didn't take long for word to get around the IHL that when you grabbed Laird, you wished you hadn't.''

Laird was like that from the very first time he stepped onto the ice as a Komet. After practicing with the team for about 10 days, Laird finally got his chance in late November, 1974, when coach Teddy Wright sent him out.

``That first game was against Columbus, and I remember coming off the bench getting right after it,'' Laird said. ``I had a big hit.''

Laird's love affair with Fort Wayne was almost as instantaneous. He still remembers his first day at practice, especially the number of fans who were watching from the stands.

``When you go to the rink and practice, there were fans there, and you really felt like you wanted to perform here,'' Laird said. ``I could not wait to get on the ice. It was a real connection. I was excited to be here and the fans were responsive.''

Laird finished his rookie season with 15 goals and 43 points and 115 penalty minutes in 62 games, but the Komets did not make the playoffs. They would the next year and every other year Laird was affiliated with the team, either as a player or coach.

They got a head start the next year when center Terry McDougall was acquired from the Des Moines Capitals in a dispersal draft. McDougall was a supremely talented playmaker who was used to winning.

``I came down a couple of weeks early just to get some ice and skate,'' Laird said. ``We're staying at the Sands Hotel, and the first guy I run into was Dugie. We had played against each other in juniors, and had a couple of words and decided we'd go for a beer."

They ended up rooming together during training camp and then getting an apartment together once the season started. Then coach Ralph Keller put the duo together on a line with veteran D'Arcy Keating. They were successful immediately, as Laird scored 30 goals for the first of six times as a Komet and finished with 68 points. McDougall scored 35 goals and 88 points, and Keating had 26 goals and a career-high 67 points.

The next season, Laird's former Regina teammate Al Dumba showed up and replaced Keating. Noting that Laird and Dumba were from Saskatchewan and McDougall from British Columbia, Gallmeier dubbed them ``The Western Union Line." They were an immediate success as McDougall scored 36 goals and 102 points in 1976-77, setting up Laird for 43 goals and 89 points and Dumba for 31 goals and 63 points.

``There was a real connection with Dugie on and off the ice," Laird said. ``On the ice, it was just one of those things. The puck would come to me on a breakout or on the boards or a pass, and I wouldn't be looking at Dugie, I'd be looking at the puck but I always knew where he was. He read me pretty good, too. I think that's where a lot of our offense started, leaving our zone on the breakout. Dugie would carry the puck through the middle of the ice, making plays, and it was usually me going to the net. Al was a good shooter, D'Aarcy was a good shooter. We really had some different ingredients that made it successful here, but Dugie certainly was the key guy. He had the most skills by a long way."

The Western Union Line was just getting started. In 1977-78, they had what would have been a good season for any other line but only a hint of what they would later accomplish. McDougall scored 36 goals and 84 points, Dumba had 31 goals and 94 points, but Laird slipped to 20 goals and 42 points, mostly because of nagging injuries. He basically played the entire second half with a broken foot.

With a healthy Laird back stirring things up in the corners and in front of the net, in 1978-79 the line produced one of the most remarkable seasons in Fort Wayne and International Hockey League history. Laird scored 45 goals and 102 points, Dumba 46 goals and 111 points and McDougall led the league with 57 goals and 139 points to tie Len Thornson's franchise record.

At the end of the season, they became the first and eventually only line in IHL history to have all three members named to the first-team all-league squad. McDougall was named the league's Most Valuable Player.

"The best years I ever had playing, the most fun and the most productive, were with Robbie on my left wing, and I played with some very good left wingers," McDougall said. "There might have been other guys who were better fundamentally and more talented, but nobody played the position better. I think he made our line better just by the way he worked so hard. If you didn't play up to his level, you were out of place and you had to keep up.

"Nobody realizes what a fighter he was, and he was unique because he could throw with both hands. They all want to grab on with one and throw with the other, but Robbie could throw with either hand. He surprised a lot of six-footers that way. He's score 45 goals, 100 points and earn 300 penalty minutes – I'd take that on my left wing any day."

It turned out to be the Western Union Line's last season, though McDougall scored 93 points the next year and Dumba was the league's MVP with 47 goals and 119 points in 1979-80. The summer before Laird finally got a good break from an NHL team and left Fort Wayne.

``It was always my dream to play in the NHL, but I really wasn't thinking about it," Laird said. ``Once you've been in the IHL back then for three or four years, I thought they kind of forgot about me. But then I got a call over the summer from the Minnesota North Stars by the coach and general manager, Glen Somner and Lou Nanne. Eventually, they gave me a deal. They said we want to sign you to an NHL contract. It was what I had been dreaming about, but it wasn't an easy thing to leave Fort Wayne. I loved playing here, but a chance to get an NHL contract, I jumped on it."

The Stars' farm team was in Oklahoma City of the Central Hockey League so that's where Laird was assigned, playing there for two years and then another in Nashville when the franchise moved.

The move paid off almost immediately. Because he had stayed in Fort Wayne that summer, Laird had not seen his parents for more than a year when they came to visit in Oklahoma City. After watching Robbie play in a game the night before, the Lairds were catching up the next night as Robbie's phone was ringing back in his apartment. The Stars had an injured player and needed Laird the next night for a game against Vancouver. By the time he got home and got the message, it was 12:30 a.m. and he had a 6 a.m. flight to catch.

He walked into the Minnesota locker room in time to play a regular shift in the first period. He wore No. 31.

``My first shift I had a pretty good scoring opportunity," he said. ``The puck was dumped in and I got it and I threw it at Glen Hanlon."

The score ended 5-5 as Laird played about 10 minutes. He did not post any points.

``It wasn't a great game and now looking back I wish I had done more, at least get into a fight or something," he said. ``After the game they thanked me and they sent me back."

He didn't receive a jersey or even a picture of himself playing in the game, and his parents didn't get to see him play, either. It was the only time Laird was called up to the NHL that season and in his entire career, though the Stars did let him hang around of the team during their Stanley Cup run that spring.

``They gave me an opportunity and that's all I can ask," he said. ``It just all happened so darn quickly and out of the blue. I wish it had been under different circumstances, but there's no sense looking back. I got my game and it was a bit of a life-long achievement anyways."

Unfortunately for Laird, that was about the only good thing to happen to him on the ice for a few years. Because of injuries, he played only 55 games the next season in Oklahoma City and then only 35 in 1981-

82 in Nashville. For a player who had always taken pride in playing through injuries – even once playing in more than 200 straight games – this was a particularly difficult time.

``I had a groin injury the end of my second year at Oklahoma City and I tried to rehab it all summer," Laird said. ``I saw all kinds of therapists, massage therapists, doctors. It was a hockey hernia and they couldn't discover it. I finally ended up having surgery before going to camp and it was just an upper stomach hernia. I missed the first part of the season because my groins weren't ready, and I couldn't get them right that entire year. It was really frustrating for me because I could play at about 80 percent, and that wasn't good enough for me. I wasn't very effective. I said, I can't play."

About the only good thing that happened to him during that time was he married Victoria Smith of Fort Wayne. They had met through mutual friends a couple years before.

``She knew I was training hard in the summer time leading up to training camp, but she didn't know anything about hockey," he said. ``So it was an exhibition game, she shows up walking around the lower corridor, and she hears people banging on the glass, and there I was in a fight. It freaked her out. She said, `What kind of barbaric sport are you playing?' That's what she said, I remember the words. What kind of barbaric sport is this? She ended up getting used to it and was a good hockey wife."

She had to be after Laird's injuries continued, and at age 27 in 1982, he retired to return to Fort Wayne. He thought his career was over. Former Komets Eddie Long, George Drysdale and George Polinuk helped him get a job with AALCO Distributing as a wine distributor. The job gave him some assurance that if he wasn't playing hockey, at least there was something he could do.

But he also realized it wasn't what he wanted to do with the rest of his life. Luckily, the time off from hockey was having some good effect on his groin injuries. He started working on stretching exercises and played racquetball at the YMCA, and finally started to feel better around December that year. Laird and asked Komets coach Ron Ullyot for some advice on physical fitness, and Ullyot gave him a program former Komet Tommie McVie developed. Laird tore into it with his usual passion.

Finally feeling good, that summer Laird talked to Ullyot about coming back to the Komets. When he showed up in training camp, Laird dominated all of Ullyot's physical fitness tests. He had also changed his skating stride to help avoid further injuries.

By that time McDougall had been traded to Flint and Dumba had retired, but the IHL continued to improve.

``When I first came to this league, I realized the IHL was a very under-appreciated league and a much better league than the hockey world gave it credit for," Laird said. ``To be honest with you, when you were playing junior hockey, junior would be bigger than the IHL. You always thought it was the AHL and the Central, and a lot of guys wouldn't go to the IHL. A lot of guys would get drafted and sent here but they couldn't play in this league because it was too rough for them.

``It was very much a man's league when I first came here, very much a physical league. At that time in the early 70s, the Philadelphia Flyers were having success and that's the way hockey was played. So it was crazy, and a lot of guys would not hang around. It went from that level and then when I came back my second time around they had the Salt Lakes and the travel got to be a little bit more. The caliber of play was probably as good or better, and teams could send their higher prospects here."

He came back to score 37 goals and 83 points in 1983-84 and 33 goals and 67 points in 1984-85. One of his last games was one of his best. The Komets won the first three games of a first-round playoff series against Salt Lake before losing the next three games to force a Game 7 in Fort Wayne. With his team facing the possible humiliation of blowing a 3-0 series lead, Laird scored a hat trick and had two assists as the Komets won 6-2.

Another positive thing that happened during the 1984-85 season was the birth of his daughter Vanessa. One of her baby pictures shows her father, sporting a pair of black eyes from a fight, holding her while wearing the hospital gown.

After helping the Komets win the IHL regular-season title in 1984-85, he decided to retire as a player for good at the end of that season. Laird knew his body had gone through enough even though he had been in phenomenal shape. He was 30 years old.

Laird had met Bob Benhower of Nob Brick that spring and started work driving a forklift and grabbing rocks off trucks to stack them. He thought it was time to get on with his life away from hockey, but there was a surprise coming.

Then Ullyot shocked everyone by leaving the Komets to take a job with the Indianapolis Checkers and a chance to work with the New York Islanders' affiliate. Laird heard the news and decided to take a long shot and tell Komets Owner Colin Lister he was interested in the job. Though he had no formal experience, Laird had attended a few coaching seminars over the years and had worked at summer hockey schools for almost a decade.

``I wasn't ready for a job, and it was going to be learning on the job," Laird said, ``Colin was looking for somebody with more experience, but he had enough faith in me to give me the job. It was on the job training that first year which is the most critical time, but we had a good year."

It was especially good considering he was coaching former teammates such as Doug Rigler, Wally Schreiber, Ron Leef, Jim Burton, Steve Salvucci, Craig Channell and Dale Baldwin.

``Going from player to coach, you wonder how that transition is going to occur, but I thought it went pretty smoothly, actually," Laird said. ``I don't think I was a heavy, but I was able to have some discipline, largely because we had some real good character people on our team. There were some tough times where I had to trade or let a guy go that I had played with before. I tried to spin it into a positive."

And Laird wasn't completely done as a player. When the Komets were hit hard by injuries during his first season behind the bench, Laird activated himself on December 8, 1985. In a game against Toledo, Laird came off the bench to fight Toledo tough guy Chris McSorley during a 6-5 Fort Wayne win.

``That's when the game turned around," Laird said. ``When I got kicked out, we got going. I guess they wanted to get me off the ice."

After trailing 5-1 early, the Komets were down 5-3 at the time but rallied to win in a shootout.

Two days later, Laird was suspended by the IHL for one game. He played again December 12 against Flint, but then his three-game tryout contract expired and he needed to clear waivers before he could sign another. Fearing the possibility of facing Laird as a player in the playoffs, Milwaukee General Manager Phil Wittliff claimed Laird for the $200 waiver price, effectively ending his playing career.

``Laird is the kind of guy who would come on the ice and respond to the situation," Wittliff said. ``And with him on the ice, his players would respond as well. I didn't want him scoring the winning goal against us in the playoffs."

``I was a little flattered, but mostly I was surprised," Laird said. ``He must have been going off my past record and not my performance in those two games."

Those two games meant Laird finished his Komets playing career with 577 games, 251 goals, 305 assists, 556 points and 1,298 penalty minutes to rank in the top 10 of the franchise's all-time lists in each category.

Back behind the bench, the 1985-86 season was a remarkable one on the ice as the Komets went 52-22-8 to win the Huber Trophy as the IHL's regular-season champions. They lost to Muskegon in the Turner Cup Finals.

Lister later took great pride in Laird's success, and was thrilled that he was the one who gave him a chance. It turned out to be the best thing that happened to the Komets during the most turbulent time in the team's long history. While everything was going wrong with the business, Laird's teams won 52, 48, 48 and 46 games.

``Robbie more or less sold himself," Lister said. ``I was told I should go after somebody with experience, but Robbie kept telling me how much he wanted the opportunity to coach the Komets and that he could do the job. I wouldn't say it was his persistence – that would have turned me off. I guess he just talked his way into the job."

There were two problems, though. Attendance continued to slip, and the Komets were never able to go all the way during the playoffs. Lister eventually sold part of the team to Bob Britt who had to declare bankruptcy in 1986. That's when David Welker bought the team out of bankruptcy court for $300,000 after RediMed had bid $250,000. The court declared that because Welker wasn't a hockey person he needed one, and Laird was immediately retained as coach.

Welker was a flamboyant owner who had so many ideas he couldn't try them all or focus on any long enough for them to work. Laird maintained control of the on-ice product throughout the changeover.

``David gave me a great big office that I was a little bit humbled by," Laird said. ``It worked out fine. There were obviously some crazy moments, but I was too wrapped up in the job to really pay too much attention. I was wrapped up in what I had to do."

He was also pretty busy off the ice as he and Victoria welcomed son Grant during the 1988-89 season.

While he was coaching the Komets, one of Laird's responsibilities was to find NHL affiliations which led him to developing a relationship with the Washington Capitals and Jack Button who had scouted Laird as a player. Button spent a great deal of time in Fort Wayne evaluating players, and getting to know Laird as a coach. When Washington coach Brian Murray needed an assistant, Button recommended Laird, who always dreamed of becoming an NHL head coach.

Laird left the Komets after the 1988-89 season, but it turned out he was Murray's assistant for only a short time. After spending training camp in Europe, the tired Capitals got off to a terrible start and Murray was fired, only to be replaced by his brother Terry who had been coaching Washington's farm team in Baltimore. After the switch, the Capitals ended up turning things around and advanced as far as the Eastern Conference Finals that season.

The next year Washington asked Laird to take over Baltimore. The Skipjacks made the playoffs in Laird's first year, but a slow start led to Laird being replaced by assistant Barry Trotz in the second season. It turned out he wasn't the problem as the Skipjacks finished the season 5-12-3 after Laird was replaced.

``That was probably my most regrettable year in coaching," Laird said. ``That was certainly my low point to that point and time."

Also that summer, he and Victoria divorced.

Laird bounced back professionally in part because of a relationship he started in Fort Wayne with the Winnipeg Jets who regularly sent the Komets a goaltender. General Manager Mike Smith hired him to coach the Jets' farm team in Moncton. The Hawks made the playoffs in Laird's first year of 1992-93, but again got off to a slow start the next season. This time Laird did not get fired, but the Hawks made a few trades and got hot in the second half. They won three playoff rounds before losing to goaltender Olie Kolzig and Portland.

That summer, the Jets decided they could not afford a farm team and decided to share a squad in Springfield, meaning Laird was again looking for work, and once again his Fort Wayne connections came into play. This time Adam Keller, the brother of former Komets coach Ralph Keller, called to ask Laird to coach the Los Angeles Kings' farm team in Phoenix.

Laird was able to bring a few players with him, and the Roadrunners finished 41-26-14 in his first season. Though he had a reputation in Fort Wayne for coaching a defensive style, the Roadrunners were much more offensive and wide open as Laird adjusted to the players he had. During his second season there, the Roadrunners finished 36-35-11. One thing he enjoyed the most about coaching the Roadrunners was his annual trip to Fort Wayne.

``I want to do well there," he said in 1995. ``I loved to play there and loved to coach there. My motivation was the fans and the people of Fort Wayne. Even though I'm coaching a different team, there's pride at stake and, and I want our team to come up with a good game."

They usually did, beating the Komets three of five times in Fort Wayne over Laird's three-year tenure in Phoenix.

In the summer of 1996 the Kings asked Laird if he'd like to become a scout with the team, and he accepted, but that didn't last long. After the Roadrunners got off to a 4-18-4 start, the Kings asked Laird to return on Dec. 6. Ironically, he'd been forced to rebuff any potential advances by the Komets a few weeks before when they were searching for a new coach. He led the Roadrunners to a 23-26-9 mark and they almost made the playoffs.

That completed Laird's coaching career with a 424-328-97 record, including 294-195-60 in the IHL. Then Laird returned to scouting for good.

``I could have continued coaching, but the kids were living in Fort Wayne and here I am in Phoenix," he said. ``The kids would come out and I'd try to make it back, but it was just really difficult. I decided to stay in pro scouting so I could have a little more control of my visits. Certainly I didn't achieve my goal of coaching in the NHL as a head coach, but this is what I needed to do."

It was around that time that he met Madeleine Simon who was the general manager of the Phoenix Cobras, a new indoor roller hockey team. They got married in 2000 and moved to Fort Wayne soon after.

Throughout his career after he left Fort Wayne, Laird continued to keep close ties with the Komets, mostly through his friendships with broadcaster Bob Chase, former assistant Al Sims and with the Franke brothers. Sometimes he'd recommend a rookie the team should check out and he also provided his thoughts on potential coaches when asked. Occasionally he'd stop by the coliseum to scout a game and once even scouted for the Komets during the playoffs when he was out of work.

``Robbie Laird was an incredible coach and an incredible player," Chase said. ``He's one of the highlights of my life in this town. To watch him come from a rookie who came in here with a broken hand and he couldn't even play when it all got started to see what he has done with his life and his hockey career, that's an incredible success story."

As the Kings' pro scout, Laird is responsible for evaluating every player in the NHL, AHL and throughout Europe, adding his input on trades, free agent signings and waiver pickups. He watches more than 150 games a year.

``You are also comparing guys by birth date because players become free agents at certain times," he said. ``You're looking at guys who you want for prospects down the road, depth players, maybe somebody you want for your own minor league team."

In 2006, after some changes in Kings' management, Laird considered leaving the organization, but Los Angeles proved how valuable they thought he was by answering all his needs. He has second-most seniority of all but one person in the hockey department.

His ultimate goal has changed from coaching in the NHL to helping a team win a Stanley Cup and maybe moving up to become a director of player personnel. He no longer feels the tug to coach but doesn't want to move too high up in management so that he's further from the ice. He might consider an assistant general manager position if he could focus on the hockey side of the business.

Despite the short interludes working at AALCO and Knob Brick, Laird has been able to continue working in hockey virtually his entire life. He still loves and respects the game and is extremely grateful for all it has given him.

`` I was always motivated to be a hockey player because there was nothing else I wanted to do or knew I could do and I did whatever it took to remain in hockey," he said. ``I never thought about doing anything else. I think I was motivated a little bit by fear. What would I have done if I wasn't playing hockey?"

And hockey led him to Fort Wayne and in many ways kept pulling him back here.

Moving to Fort Wayne allowed Laird to spend more time with his children. Vanessa is going to school at Humboldt State in northern California where she studies environmental technology and the arts, and in 2007 Grant graduated from Homestead High School where he played football and wrestled.

``I've never been more emotionally involved in a game, even when I played, than when they played Snider in the sectional (in 2006)," he said. ``They hadn't beaten Snider in eight or nine years and they beat them in the sectional. I had to think a long time back as a coach and as a player to when I was so wrapped up in a game. It was a great game."

He and Madeleine have talked about moving back to Phoenix, but Laird says he'd still maintain a home in Fort Wayne. After all, this place is his home.

``The people are what made Fort Wayne so special," he said. ``It wasn't the money, you know that. What motivates me the most is people appreciating what you do, and that's what happened from Day 1 here. That is what really motivated me to keep trying to play the game at the highest level.

``Coming to Fort Wayne has been very rewarding for me in a lot of ways. It gave me the opportunity to develop many relationships and friendships with some very special people. It has allowed me to pursue the only profession I ever thought about and remain in it. For that, coming to Fort Wayne was a great move for me and I count my blessings."

One of those blessings was having his number 18 retired on Nov. 6, 2004. The first thing he did was thank the fans.

Robbie Laird's career statistics Playing Regular season*Playoffs

Season	Team	League	GP	G	A	PTS	PIM	GP	G	A	PTS	PIM
74-75	Fort Wayne	IHL	62	15	28	43	115	*	*	*	*	*
75-76	Fort Wayne	IHL	78	30	38	68	9	8	4	12	15	*
76-77	Fort Wayne	IHL	78	43	46	89	151	9	3	3	6	10
77-78	Fort Wayne	IHL	64	29	22	42	202	11	3	6	9	46
78-79	Fort Wayne	IHL	80	45	62	107	13	7	10	17	80	*
79-80	Okla. City	CHL	61	26	19	45	160	*	*	*	*	*
79-80	Minnesota	NHL	1	0	0	0	0	*	*	*	*	*
80-81	Okla. City	CHL	55	24	23	47	137	3	1	1	2	8
81-82	Nashville	CHL	35	5	13	18	55	3	0	1	1	15
83-84	Fort Wayne	IHL	77	37	46	83	137	4	0	1	1	17
84-85	Fort Wayne	IHL	79	33	34	67	157	7	5	12	25	*
85-86	Fort Wayne	IHL	2	0	0	0	15	*	*	*	*	*

Coaching

Season	Team	League	GP	W-L-T	PTS	Playoffs
85-86	Fort Wayne	IHL	82	52-22-8	112	lost in finals
86-87	Fort Wayne	IHL	82	48-26-8	104	lost in semifinals
87-88	Fort Wayne	IHL	82	48-30-4	100	lost in quarterfinals
88-89	Fort Wayne	IHL	82	46-30-6	98	lost in semifinals
89-90	Washington	NHL		assistant coach		
90-91	Baltimore	AHL	80	39-34-7	85	lost in first round
91-92	Baltimore	AHL	60	23-30-7	53	*
92-93	Moncton	AHL	80	31-33-16	78	lost in first round
93-94	Moncton	AHL	80	37-36-7	81	lost in conference finals
94-95	Phoenix	IHL	81	41-26-14	96	lost in semifinals
95-96	Phoenix	IHL	60	23-30-7	*	*

STEVE FLETCHER

CHAPTER 12

Practice ended 45 minutes earlier, but seven Komets are standing around listening to retired Komet Steve Fletcher talk the art of hockey fights. It's the dog days of the season and usually they'd be heading for lunch, but today if they had pen and paper, they'd all be writing furiously.

``When I played, I'd do whatever I had to do for the team," Fletcher tells the players. "You make sacrifices. You don't have to be the toughest guy to get the team going. You can change a hockey game. When the team is down two goals, that's the time to go. If your guys are down or they're dead on the bench, you get a good fight and boom, you can get them going. Sometimes all it takes is a few good hits, one guy wakes up and maybe that wakes another guy up and it's a domino effect.

``Every game is important and you are there to win. If you know it and see it, it's all about the team because if they don't start winning, they are going to start getting rid of guys. Sometimes you have to sacrifice and put your emotions into the game. You can change a game."

By making those sacrifices and fighting for his team and fighting back, Fletcher changed more than a few games, and he helped turn around the entire Fort Wayne franchise in 1990-91. Then he fought to keep the Komets playing to a high standard. No one could fire up the Komets or the Memorial Coliseum crowd like Fletcher, of whom Bruce Boudreau once said, ``When Fletchie dresses, the whole team plays bigger."

Steven Craig Fletcher was born March 31, 1962 in Montreal to Lorenzo Rolf "Bobby" Fletcher and Marguerite Fletcher. He worked for Canadian Pacific Railroad, and she was a telephone operator.

Considering how Fletcher's career later developed, the start was completely unremarkable. He didn't learn to skate until age 10 and rarely played sports before that. He even joined his first hockey team late in the season, playing on an older Pee Wee C level squad because it needed replacements for some injured players.

``We played on an outside rink, and you were always hoping you were on the right side so you weren't facing the blizzard for two periods, but just one," Fletcher said, laughing. ``Once we played in a tournament indoors, and I wondered what I had to do to play in there because we were freezing outdoors. The referee would call time out and we'd all go in to warm up and come back out. Somebody told me I had to get good enough that a team that played inside would want me."

That was his last season playing outside, but Fletcher's early calling wasn't hockey, but baseball where he was a hard-throwing pitcher who was later ranked as the top thrower in Quebec. He had been an outfielder when one day his team was getting blitzed. Knowing Fletcher had a good arm, the coach put him in to pitch, and then left him in even though the score eventually reached 34-7.

``If I wasn't walking hitters or hitting them, they'd be hitting me," Fletcher said. ``My talent was in baseball and my heart was in hockey."

As Fletcher continued to develop as a pitcher, the Montreal Expos kept tabs on him, but hockey wouldn't let him go. Fletcher improved quickly as a defenseman, though he figured his career would end when he completed midget play. He was quite surprised when Hull drafted him into juniors.

That's probably because Fletcher weighed only 164 pounds at age 17 heading into his first junior season. It wasn't until a couple of years later that he hit a growth spurt, eating everything in sight and working out by doing pushups to increase to 195 pounds over a six-month period. Fletcher also quit playing baseball but not before reconsidering.

During his first year of pro hockey, Fletcher was sick of fighting basically every game and told his mother he would quit at the end of the season and go back to baseball. Before that could happen he threw his shoulder out fighting Dave Brown, ending any baseball hopes. Luckily, his reputation as a fighter was established during his first three seasons and Fletcher didn't have to scrap as much the next two seasons.

Though his junior numbers were solid but not spectacular, at the end of his third season his coach told Fletcher he needed an agent. Fletcher wasn't buying it. In fact, on draft day, Fletcher was sitting at home when his friend John Chabot was drafted by the Canadiens. After Chabot called Fletcher to come get him so they could go out and celebrate, Fletcher walked into the Forum to shake Chabot's hand. Then he heard over the public address system, ``The Calgary Flames select defenseman Steve Fletcher from Hull Olympics." The most shocked guy in the place was the 202nd overall pick in the 10th round.

Fletcher hired an agent who was basically incompetent and gave up after getting a busy signal the first time he called the Flames. Fletcher didn't find out until the Flames called after the start of training camp wanting to know where he was. A year later Calgary dropped his rights.

The general manager of the American Hockey League's Sherbrooke Jets heard Fletcher's story and signed him in 1982. Fletcher played 36 games with the Jets, but the team needed to ship someone out and Fletcher was sent to Fort Wayne of the International Hockey League.

``When I first came here, I'm hearing things from the guys that it was like 'Slapshot,' " Fletcher said. ``Early on we're playing here against Kalamazoo and Leefer (Ron Leef) got cross checked at center ice and he's out cold. I look over and all of a sudden Hilworth throws his gloves up in the air and dove over the bench, and I'm going, 'Oh, man, I'm in the 'I.' I want to go home.' "

But like his first season in junior, the 34 games Fletcher played in Fort Wayne showed his continual improvement. He teamed mostly with Wayne Bishop on defense, lived with George Kotsopoulos, partied with John Hilworth and learned everything he could from Dale Baldwin.

``He used to work out all the time," Fletcher said. "I never saw Baldy fight anybody who was ever smaller than him. Pound for pound, he was one of the toughest I've ever seen. He pretty much babysat me."

When Fletcher returned to Sherbrooke for training camp the next season, he was one of the team's most improved players and he played a career-high 77 games. Sherbrooke had a great team led by twin brothers Perry and Paul Pooley. When opponents started pounding on the Pooleys, the coach asked Fletcher to switch from defense to their left wing. After scoring three points in his first five games, he stayed on the line throughout the playoffs.

Exclusively playing forward the next season, Fletcher scored two goals and 14 points in 64 games with 293 penalty minutes. His reward was his first NHL contract, signing with Montreal. Unfortunately, there wasn't much to celebrate. After a good training camp, Fletcher was told he made the team one day and then sent to Sherbrooke the next. Montreal wanted him to drop 15 pounds to get to 212, telling him he'd be back within two weeks.

Fletcher dropped to 212 in two weeks, but the call never came. Though the Canadiens didn't seem to want Fletcher, they also didn't want anyone else to have him, either. At the same time, Pittsburgh was trying to trade for Fletcher, but Montreal's asking price was too high. Instead, Fletcher stayed in Sherbrooke and put together his best offensive season, scoring 15 goals and 26 points in 70 games with 261 penalty minutes. He was hot right from the start of the season.

``We were playing an exhibition game, and I got two goals which was as many as I scored the whole previous year," Fletcher said. "One of the sports guys was interviewing me and asked how many goals I was going to get that year, so I said, 'I don't know, five.' He said, 'You know what, Fletch, for every five goals you get, I'm going to buy you a bottle of champagne.' I said no problem, and then I scored 15 goals in the regular season and another six in the playoffs."

It was good champagne, but it also led to another story. When Fletcher was growing up, he played baseball against Gord Donnelly and the two became best friends. They were talking on the phone early that season.

``You're on fire," Donnelly said. ``You know what, you score 20 goals I'm going to kiss your (behind) on St. Catherine's Street in downtown Montreal."

After that season, Fletcher called Donnelly up to tell him he had scored 21 goals. One day the duo and Donnelly's girlfriend were driving through Montreal when Donnelly stopped the car.

``I'm paying my bet off right now," Donnelly said.

``We got out and it took us about 20 minutes to do it because we were laughing so hard," Fletcher said. ``It was hilarious, but he did it."

Fletcher came back the next year to set career-highs with 29 points and 338 penalty minutes, but again the Canadiens ignored him – until the playoffs. With his team getting whipped by Boston in the 1988 Adams Division finals, Montreal coach Jean Perron brought Fletcher up in an act of desperation.

On Fletcher's first shift he fought the Bruins' Lyndon Byers, or rather, Byers fought him.

``We were in a commercial break, and the next thing you know his gloves were down and he was jumping on my back," Fletcher said. ``I was bent over getting ready for the face-off, not even paying attention. He never hit me in the face or hurt me because I was able to defend myself."

It took Fletcher five years go get Byers back. During the 1993-94 season when Byers was playing for Las Vegas, Fletcher challenged Byers to a fight before a face-off in Las Vegas. Byers pretended he wasn't paying attention and then jumped Fletcher again. Fletcher won the fight, but wasn't happy so he wanted a rematch on March 9, 1994, in Fort Wayne, Fletcher told Komets coach Bruce Boudreau what was going on, and Boudreau said, ``Do whatever you have to."

Fletcher grabbed Byers from behind, swung him around and started throwing, earning the first and only instigation penalty of his 14-year career. In the penalty box Byers yelled that he couldn't believe Fletcher had jumped him, and Fletcher couldn't believe Byers didn't remember and kept pointing to his back.

``I never wanted anybody to say I jumped them," Fletcher said. ``I wanted a fair fight all the time, because I didn't want to hear any excuses after I beat you. I never ran, I stood up for whatever was coming."

The playoff game turned out to be the only time Fletcher played for the Canadiens, and it was the last game he ever played for the Montreal organization. During that summer, a friend of Fletcher's heard a representative of the Canadiens' front office derogatorily mention the color of Fletcher's skin. When Fletcher found out about that, he told his agent he wanted out of Montreal.

Fletcher was born a mulatto but he considered his racial makeup to matter about as much as his shoe size.

``I never thought about it,'' he said. ``When I grew up, my neighborhood was mixed. I played baseball and hockey with everybody. We had everything, Jewish, black, white, French, Filipino. I never thought anything of it.''

That doesn't mean that Fletcher didn't have to deal with race. There were several incidents over the years, particularly some early ones in Indianapolis. The lesson Fletcher took from those were numerous letters from Ice fans apologizing for the behavior of others.

After leaving the Canadiens, Fletcher signed a three-year contract with Winnipeg. He was with the Jets for 10 games in 1988-89, dressing for three and making his National Hockey League regular-season debut on October 14, 1988 against Vancouver. The Jets were struggling and sent Fletcher to their AHL farm team in Moncton and in December traded him to Philadelphia for future considerations.

The Flyers assigned Fletcher to Hershey, where Fletcher's career seemed to be dying. The Bears' coach told him to stop fighting, and then quit putting him the lineup, even though he scored 13 points in 29 games. The fans started complaining, wearing ``Fletch Lives'' T-shirts. After playing only 28 games in 1989-90, Fletcher's contract was over and he was a free agent,

By this time, Fletcher's outlook was as bleak has his career prospects. He was 28 years old but felt cheated after playing only 83 games on four teams over the past two seasons. Because he kept himself in exceptional shape, Fletcher knew he could still play if he got the chance. All he needed was a fresh start and an honest opportunity.

His agent was trying to set that up in a deal with the San Diego Gulls, but Fletcher ended up coming to Fort Wayne on a tryout instead. A Flyers official had told Komets coach Al Sims that Fletcher was on his way out of the game, and that he didn't want to fight any more, but Sims soon found out Fletcher was hungry to prove that was a lie.

"He was one of the toughest guys in the league, and it wasn't only his toughness, but he could play," Sims said. "I think he enjoyed his role. He loved being the tough guy. I know a lot of battles we had against Indy and Kalamazoo, if we hadn't had Steve Fletcher, we would not have won championships and done the things we did. Nobody wants to be a fighter, bruising up your face and hands all the time, but Fletch stepped up to the plate every time."

The move to Fort Wayne revitalized Fletcher's career as he helped revitalize the Komets. After starting them on different lines, Sims paired Fletcher with Robin Bawa and Kevin "Killer" Kaminski early in the season, forming the Ice Patrol. They were known for their fists, but they were also an exceptional defensive line and Sims regularly paired them against the opponents' top line. Opposing players were often more worried about where the Ice Patrol was rather than what they were supposed to be doing with the puck.

Hoping the trio would play one or two shifts per period like most tough guys, a wary opponent once asked Bawa how long his line would be matched up against the Ice Patrol.

``All night long," Bawa replied.

And the line took over games. When they skated onto the ice at the start of a shift, the crowd couldn't wait to see what would happen. It seemed like every shift something would, usually a fight. Kaminski finished with a team-record 455 penalty minutes, Bawa earned 381 and Fletcher 289. There had never been another line like it in Komets' history.

``Killer had two bandits on his side, and I knew I had coverage," Fletcher said. "Pound for pound he was a tough little guy. We clicked just like that. They knew they were going to get hit and they hated it. We'd dump it in and chase it and guys would hear footsteps. I'd be like `I'm coming' and they'd be looking over their shoulders."

Defensemen Mike Butters also earned 216 minutes and Tom Karalis 239 as the Komets turned Memorial Coliseum into ``The Jungle."

After several seasons in decline, the Komets were the hottest ticket in town, especially after the team pulled off a pair of playoff upsets to reach the Turner Cup Finals. That squad became the all-time favorite team of many Komets fans.

``No one expected it but we believed in ourselves and we were just a hard-nosed hockey team," Fletcher said. ``We weren't fancy, we didn't pat ourselves on the back, we just went out there and were hungry to win. When you have 18, 19 hungry guys, that's a dangerous team."

The next season Kaminski and Bawa left to sign NHL contracts so Fletcher remained as the heavyweight champ, now teaming with Craig Martin, Chris McRae and Scott Shaunessy. Fletcher's reputation meant he faced challenges every night from up and coming fighters hoping to build their own reputation. Other times veterans just wanted a shot at him.

``It's amazing how fast word carries out there," Fletcher said. "Everybody knows everybody and has played with somebody on other teams, and boom, that word goes out. I wasn't the best of fighters, but I was the kind of guy if I didn't think I did right, I'll see you again and again. I was never scared of anyone. I'll keep coming after you. I'll make it a very long day because I have all the time in the world."

Fletcher also never gave cheap shots because he didn't want to hear any excuses when the fight was over. He was always willing to go head-to-head anytime, and he could tell if someone was all show and no go. There were memorable battles over the years with foes such as Mark Major, Kerry Clark, Enrico Ciccone, Jeff Buchanan, Denny Lambert, Jason Simon, Kevin Evans, Rick Hayward, Tony Twist, Mike Peluso, Tony Horacek and Kerry Toporowski. The wars with Toporowski lasted for a couple years and included several ugly incidents and ended up getting both players banned in the other team's city.

As much as opponents hated Fletcher, his teammates always did and still do love him.

"The guy prepared for every game like it was his last game," Kelly Hurd said. "He was always ready to play, always chomping at the bit to get out there."

Part of Fletcher's pre-game routine included rubbing his legs down with Icy Hot. He also had a stick with eight pucks taped to the blade that he would swing around to loosen his wrists. One time he caught teammate Carey Lucyk right before a game, and the cut required stitches. Fletcher also used to put Vaseline on his face before fights.

"He was real quirky in the dressing room," Hurd said. "You'd have thought he was a 50-goal scorer the way he prepared his sticks, spending so much time, getting them just perfect. He spent more time on them then guys like Scott Gruhl. I don't know if he was sharpening them up for Toporowski or what he was doing."

The amazing thing is Fletcher's shot was so hard and his stick was curved just right that his shot would curve the longer it carried. Teammates were always trying to get him to blast one from the blue line or red line just see what would happen.

Fletcher was always ready to go in part because he would drink quarts of coffee and Mountain Dew before games. So wired he couldn't keep still while standing for the national anthem, Fletcher would flex his legs and roll his head and shoulders, leading some appreciative fans to mimic his movements.

Despite all the caffeine, Fletcher said he never had any problems sleeping, partly because he was exhausted from losing so much weight during games. While playing Game 7 of the 1991 playoffs against Indianapolis, Fletcher's weight dropped from 212 pounds to 199. Today he has one cup of coffee in the morning to wake up and that's it.

Also amazingly, asides from the usual cuts and bruises, Fletcher never suffered any serious injuries from his fights, not even a broken nose. (The only time he broke his nose, Fletcher was 19 playing Frisbee football.) His hands might get cut up a little and would tighten up in the cold, but he'd stick them into hot wax to loosen them up again.

The only time he came close to suffering something serious was in a 1994 fight against Detroit's John Craighead. Fletcher hit the back of his head on the ice and was knocked unconscious.

He did suffer a few black eyes, including one that got him in lots of trouble. The summer following the 1991-92 season, Fletcher decided to stay in Fort Wayne instead of returning to Montreal as usual. Fletcher had been married for six years earlier and had a daughter named Natasha who was born November 28, 1986, but in the summer of 1992 he met his soulmate in Theresa Nichter. After their son Colin was born February 24, 1994, the couple was to be married April 3, 1994 following a Komets' road trip to Salt Lake. With the wedding coming up, Theresa had told him not to fight that weekend, but it didn't work out that way, thanks to a fight against Jason Simon, who nailed Fletcher with a finger to his right eye.

``I got the biggest shiner I've ever had," Fletcher said. "I remember I was sitting on the bench, and my eye was open, but I couldn't see out of it. I knew I was in trouble. I was the last guy coming off the plane, and she was waiting for me. All the guys were laughing."

In most of the wedding pictures, only Fletcher's good side can be seen.

A second son, Liam Craig, was born August 25, 2000.

Along with happiness off the ice, Fletcher continued to dominate on it during the Komets' great seasons during the early 1990s, receiving 320 penalty minutes in 1991-92, 337 in 1992-93 and 277 in 1993-94. Three times Fletcher and the Komets went to the Turner Cup Finals, winning the title in 1993. One of the crowd's loudest roars that night came when Fletcher hoisted the Turner Cup.

``He had such a presence that he could actually change the game just by being dressed and on the bench," Komets captain Colin Chin said. ``That says a lot about him. Guys could play hockey and not have to worry about the other stuff. It made some teams say, `You know what, we're not going to play a certain style tonight.' Sometimes when that happens some guys don't want to show up."

But after breaking Baldwin's Komets' record for career penalty minutes the next season, many of the good times were over for Fletcher and the Komets. Fort Wayne suffered through its worst season ever, and Fletcher was limited to 43 games and 204 penalty minutes. The highlight was a wrist shot on February 8, 1995 to shock Chicago goaltender Ray

LeBlanc and win an 11-round shootout. It was the first time Fletcher had ever participated in a shootout.

``It was either me (or reserve goaltender Peter) Inger, and he couldn't find his stick,'' Fletcher joked. ``They were telling me to use a wrist shot, so I used a wrist shot. I listened to the guys.''

His teammates mobbed Fletcher in celebration, which was a new experience. Usually the only time Fletcher got mobbed like that was when the other team was trying to chase him down. It was one of the only highlights in an awful season.

When Dave Farrish was hired to coach the Komets in 1995-96, Fletcher was signed to a 25-game tryout contract. Though Fletcher was in great shape and had cut his weight from 234 to 218 pounds, Farrish put him into the lineup for only two games. During the first, Fletcher scored two goals on October 13, 1995 (Yes, it was a Friday the 13th). They were the 68th, 69th and last goals Fletcher scored in his career.

He played for the Komets one more time, October 21 against Kansas City, fighting three times. On November 29, 1995, Fletcher's tryout contract was up and the wanted to move on. Rumors of his release swirled around Memorial Coliseum that night, but weren't confirmed until the next morning. Fletcher had totaled 1,745 penalty minutes in 325 games as a Komet with 27 goals, 64 points and countless bruises given and received.

Komets General Manager David Franke said it was the toughest decision he'd ever had to make about the club, and team President Michael Franke said, ``Steve exemplified what it means to be a Komet.''

Though Fletcher was heartbroken, he took the high road and did not respond to questions but privately felt he should have been allowed to play his way off the team. Less than a week later, Fletcher got a call from Atlanta where tough guy Brantt Myhres had suffered a broken leg, and Knights coach John Paris thought Fletcher could help.

Ironically, the signing came just as the Komets were heading to Atlanta for a two-game series. Three weeks later, just before Christmas, Fletcher was back in Fort Wayne, this time, for the first time, as the enemy.

``I came to the rink early in the morning," Fletcher said. "One of the radio guys gave me a ride to the rink because I was a bag of nerves."

He wore No. 12 because Reggie Savage had seniority on No. 77 with Atlanta (Fletcher later switched to No. 96). During the game, Fletcher fought Andy Bezeau, using his superior reach to land the first few shots against the shorter Komet. Eventually, Bezeau tackled Fletcher and threw him to the ice. Some in the Fort Wayne media made jokes about Fletcher ending up in his usual position, on his back.

``When they came down to Atlanta the following week, I beat the living crap out of him," Fletcher said, ``but that was only to prove them wrong."

Fletcher finished with 110 penalty minutes in 23 games with Atlanta, and his career seventh in the American Hockey League's all-time penalty minute list and 19th on the International Hockey League's all-time list.

The next summer, Fletcher considered playing in Europe but a couple of opportunities fell through. It was time to do something else, and he started driving a truck for RPS as a contractor. In 1999, with help from Colin Chin, Fletcher went to work with Perfection Bakery as a sales representative for the Meijer store on Maysville Road in Fort Wayne.

``Did anybody ever tell you you look like Steve Fletcher?"

Fletcher heard it all the time and usually just answered no with a smile, but eventually everyone in town knew where Fletcher worked and many would make a point to say hi early in the morning as he stocked the shelves.

To stay in hockey, Fletcher coached the Northrop High School club team. To stay in shape, he started training as a kick boxer.

But the Komets weren't done with him yet. In November, 2002, Komets President Michael Franke called to ask Fletcher to lunch. The Franke brothers never felt right about the way Fletcher's career with the Komets finished, and wanted to offer Fletcher one final game so he could retire as a Komet. He thought it would be fun for his sons to see him play.

``I think they knew that it wasn't right how things went down," Fletcher said. ``There was nothing to say, really. They talked about it for a while and we finally picked a date."

He talked with Theresa who was concerned what would happen to his day job if he was injured, so he told her he wouldn't fight. He was more likely to get hurt training to get back into shape, he said. With a month to get ready, he started practicing with the team but overdid it and strained his abdominal muscles the first day.

``I came home and iced it and I didn't skate for two weeks," Fletcher said. ``I was really wondering what was going to happen."

He was finally ready to skate for four days before playing the game on January 12, 2003. A crowd of 9,265 fans showed up to thank Fletcher with a standing ovation when he was introduced in the starting lineup. The Komets lost to Kalamazoo 2-1 in a shootout, but no one cared because the crowd got to see what it really wanted.

Kalamazoo forward Craig Billick offered to fight Fletcher in the third period. He declined, but Billick kept asking and eventually slashed Fletcher before a faceoff to send the gloves flying.

``It came back to me in seconds," Fletcher said. "All of a sudden I was a different person."

Fletcher won the fight, landing three solid blows and twice driving Billick to the ice. As their hero skated to the dressing room, the crowd roared its approval.

`` I never really got nervous in games, but I got nervous for that game," Fletcher said. ``The whole thing is timing. If you don't do it for a while and all of a sudden you are playing against guys who play every day, you could have some problems. I was proud to wear the K again and play because of the people."

A year later, on January 9, 2004, Fletcher and his fans came back once more, this time to see the No. 77 raised to the Memorial Coliseum rafters. His heart was pounding in his chest just as hard as questions were pounding in his head.

``You never think of that, it never entered my mind," Fletcher said. ``Then you wonder if you belonged with those guys. You look at all the legends up there, and you wonder if your number should be retired because there were a lot of better hockey players than I was. Things like that go through your head. I still look at it sometimes now, and it sends shivers up my spine."

Maybe that's because to this day Fletcher still can't believe that he played junior let alone professional hockey, and what the sport and Fort Wayne have meant to him. He never expected any of it and never took it for granted by always playing hard, which is partly why the fans love him so much.

Steve Fletcher's career statistics

Playing Regular season*Playoffs

Season	Team	League	GP	G	A	PTS	PIM	GP	G	A	PTS	PIM
79-80	Hull	QMJHL	61	2	14	16	183	*	*	*	*	*
80-81	Hull	QMJHL	66	4	13	17	231	*	*	*	*	*
81-82	Hull	QMJHL	60	4	20	24	230	14	1	9	10	57
82-83	Sherbrooke	AHL	36	0	1	1	119	*	*	*	*	*
82-83	Fort Wayne	IHL	34	1	9	10	115	10	1	6	7	57
83-84	Sherbrooke	AHL	77	3	7	10	208	*	*	*	*	*
84-85	Sherbrooke	AHL	50	2	4	6	192	13	0	0	0	48
85-86	Sherbrooke	AHL	64	2	12	14	293	*	*	*	*	*
86-87	Sherbrooke	AHL	70	15	11	26	261	17	6	5	11	82
87-88	Sherbrooke	AHL	76	8	21	29	338	6	2	1	3	28
87-88	Montreal	NHL	*	*	*	*	*	1	0	0	0	5

Steve Fletcher's career statistics Playing Regular season*Playoffs (continued)

Season	Team	League	GP	G	A	PTS	PIM	GP	G	A	PTS	PIM
88-89	Winnipeg	NHL	3	0	0	0	5	*	*	*	*	*
88-89	Moncton	AHL	23	1	1	2	89	*	*	*	*	*
88-89	Hershey	AHL	29	5	8	13	91	*	*	*	*	*
89-90	Hershey	AHL	28	1	1	2	132	*	*	*	*	*
90-91	Fort Wayne	IHL	66	7	9	16	289	15	2	0	2	70
91-92	Fort Wayne	IHL	60	8	3	11	320	5	0	0	0	14
92-93	Fort Wayne	IHL	54	5	6	11	337	3	0	0	0	2
93-94	Fort Wayne	IHL	47	4	6	10	277	5	0	0	0	33
94-95	Fort Wayne	IHL	43	0	2	2	204	1	0	0	0	0
95-96	Fort Wayne	IHL	2	2	0	2	39	*	*	*	*	*
95-96	Atlanta	IHL	23	0	1	1	110	*	*	*	*	*
02-03	Fort Wayne	UHL	1	0	0	0	7	*	*	*	*	*

COLIN CHIN

CHAPTER 13

Almost since he was born, Colin Chin seemed fated to become a Fort Wayne Komet. About the only person who needed convincing was Chin.

Not many people remember it, but Chin might be the youngest player ever to wear a Komets uniform on Memorial Coliseum ice during a game. Wearing a Spaceman jersey with No. 1 on it, a five-year old Chin was lifted over the boards and onto the ice by Terry Pembroke during the first intermission on opening night in 1966. The diminutive Komet wowed the crowd with his young skating skills.

``I just remember some clowns out there, and they let me shoot on the goalie," Chin said.

Even as an infant, Chin attended Komets games with his family, watching the exploits of players like Pembroke, Len Thornson, Lionel Repka and his favorite player, Chick Balon. Long-time Komets business manager and owner Colin Lister is Chin's Godfather. Even today Chin says he's seen more games from the Memorial Coliseum stands than he has from the ice.

But when Chin decided to begin a pro hockey career nearly 20 years later, he seemed like a natural fit for the Komets, but his hall of fame Fort Wayne career almost never got started.

When Chin's father Roy grew up in Jamaica, he joked that the only ice they had came in cocktail glasses. He came to Fort Wayne in 1955 to attend Indiana Tech and married his wife Sidnette in 1959. Roy was an engineer at International Harvester and Sid worked at Dana. Colin was born August 28, 1961, the first of five boys.

The Chins had season tickets behind the opposing team's bench at Komets games, and Memorial Coliseum General Manager Don

Myers constantly worried about the couple with the baby sitting there because protective glass had not been installed yet. That's why Colin loved the spot, though. Without the glass, the Chins could hear and see everything that happened on the bench and on the ice. While other kids were playing out in the hallways, Chin stayed and watched, and heard, every bit of the games.

``You could hear all the conversations, all the swearing, all the nuances of the game," Chin said. ``I got to know some of the teams and some of them let me come down to the locker room. That was probably my big attraction to it because we were so close to it."

For his third birthday, Chin received a pair of roller skates and soon showed his father how he could skate backwards, pushing off a wall and wiggling his skates. At age four, he surprised the owner at Gordie Howe's Hockeyland with his natural skating ability, and he started playing at McMillen when he was five.

Because his stepfather made him work so much in the family grocery store when he was a boy, Roy Chin made sure his sons had every opportunity to play sports as much as they wanted. When McMillen officials said a six year-old Colin was too young to play up a level in the squirt division, his father drove him to Lima where he could play against players who were two or three years older, a trend he continued throughout his developmental career. Chin scored a goal in the last game of his first season, and then another in the first game of the next season before taking off to score three or four goals each game after that.

Though he was always the youngest and smallest player on the ice, Chin was able to compete at higher levels because of his remarkable skating ability, learned from his father. Roy Chin had only started skating once Colin picked up the game, but he studied the technical side until he could teach his son and later become an International Hockey League official. While other kids were having fun during public skating at McMillen, Chin would skate for a while before his father gave him a drill to follow. Roy Chin learned the importance of skating while watching and officiating IHL games when he realized most of the players were not in the NHL because they had a weakness in their skating.

``I used to hate it, but I would do it," Colin said. ``He'd make me work on stops. Then I'd get a little bit of time to go off by myself and then I'd come back and work on stuff. If you couldn't do one thing, you had to get that right before you could do something else. A lot of kids, if they can't do one move, they'll never practice it. They won't force themselves to work on things they aren't good at, but my dad always forced me to work on things I wasn't good at."

After a couple years in Lima, the Chins returned to McMillen, playing up in the Bantam Division. During one of his first games, Chin's team won 12-0 as he scored 11 goals and assisted on the other.

During Chin's pre-teen years, he often went to Haliburton, Ontario to play in hockey camps run by the Toronto Maple Leafs. When he was 12, Chin was invited by the Maple Leafs to play for a Pee Wee team in Toronto called the Shopsy's. Chin lived with a family, and the team often practiced at historic Maple Leaf Gardens.

``It was really tough," Chin said. "I think there were a lot more expectations on me than I even realized. Here was an American kid on this high-profile team who's taking a job from some Canadian kids. I probably didn't live up to expectations."

Chin returned the next year to attend New Haven Junior High and then New Haven High School, and play with Lister's Pepsi Komets junior team. After graduating at age 17 in 1979, Chin made the Great Lakes Junior Hockey League's Paddock Pools squad out of Ecorse, Michigan. The spring before his second year, Chin was in Michigan on a family fishing trip when he heard his coach was holding a tryout for the Olympic Sports Festival. When Chin asked why he couldn't try out, the coach said this was the Michigan team and he should be trying out for the at-large team. After saying he had not received an invitation to the other tryout, Chin talked his way into a Michigan tryout and made the team. Then he played well in Oklahoma City, earning some notice from colleges.

``I took a lot of heat for being on the team because I wasn't a Michigan kid," Chin said. ``There were a lot of college kids whose parents were ticked off."

Though he weighed only 140 pounds, Chin had several offers the following year before deciding to attend Illinois-Chicago. It was a new program so there would be lots of playing time and he liked the Chicago social scene.

Because the Flames' team was just getting started, the first year was difficult and the second wasn't much better as a new coach cleaned house. One good thing happened toward the end of Chin's freshman year when he met UIC tennis player Diane Lenniger. Well, actually, he almost didn't.

``I used to hear about this beautiful girl that everybody saw working out who was on the tennis team," he said. ``This other freshman and I had seen her coming out one day so we flipped a coin to see who was going to ask her out, and I lost. The only good thing was the other guy was an idiot so I knew that wasn't going to last too long. That ran its course, and then we started dating at the end of my freshman year."

Early in his sophomore season, Chin had one of the most remarkable weekends in college hockey history. On Friday, November 12, 1982, Chin scored a hat trick against Notre Dame. The next night was even more incredible as he came back with an ``un-hat trick" by having three goals disallowed. One was for a teammate being in the crease, the second for using a high stick and the third for scoring while a penalty was being called against UIC.

By Chin's senior year, the Flames had a solid squad that climbed to No. 8 in the national rankings. In 38 games, he scored 23 goals and 65 points while his winger Ray Staszak finished as the runner-up for the Hobey Baker Award. Other stars on the team included future Komet Shawn Cronin and Mike Mersh who played some NHL games and in the IHL with Muskegon.

Because he was past NHL draft age, Chin was a free agent after his senior season but he got lucky. While he was scoring a goal and three assists against Michigan State in a late-season game, Pittsburgh Director of Player Personnel Lou Angotti was checking out another player. Instead, after the season he signed Chin, who then proposed to Diane.

The hot streak didn't last. A couple of weeks before Chin arrived in training camp, Angotti was fired. Figuring they already had three smaller players, the Penguins sent the 5-8, 160-pound Chin to their American Hockey League farm club in Baltimore.

Chin had high hopes after a fast start, but eventually his outlook changed. The Skipjacks had a talented team, but after the season the Penguins were going to break up the veterans, who quickly became complacent. The team struggled in the second half and missed the playoffs.

``After about 20 games, I was having a pretty good season," Chin said. "They were going to call a couple of guys up and I thought for sure I was going to get a chance and didn't. That and a couple of other things… You've played something all your life and it's always been for fun, but now it's all business. Looking back now, maybe I would have done some things a little differently, but I got soured on it."

One highlight was Chin's first pro fight, though it really wasn't much of a fight or a highlight. Early on in a game, Hershey goaltender Ron Hextall had taken a baseball swing at a Baltimore player so tempers were high when Chin was run by a Bears' player.

``I get up and as I'm skating away he slashes me and then he skates by me again and trips me," Chin said. ``The ref blows the whistle, and I'm thinking, `I've gotta do something' so I throw down my gloves, I skate over to him as hard as I can and I stop and he's just looking at me. He's got this look, like `What in the world are you doing?' It seemed like 20 seconds, but then he finally starts throwing and he's pounding me and then he takes two fingers and puts them in my eyeballs. I couldn't see for hours. He just beat the crap out of me. It was a learning lesson."

Most of the AHL players had come through major junior or had been in the league for a while so they were used to fighting. Coming from college hockey where fighting is prohibited, Chin was an inexperienced fighter at best. When Baltimore coach Gene Ubriaco came into the locker room, he said, ``Little, guy, you don't fight anymore."

After the season, the Penguins didn't offer him another contract which was fine with Chin. He had decided halfway through the season hockey wasn't fun any more and it was time to quit the game and start the next phase of his life. Part of that included marrying Diane on July 5, 1986. They have a daughter Taylor, born September 16, 1991 and a son Cullen born March 23, 1995.

Though the phone kept ringing with contract offers, Chin kept saying he was done. Komets coach Robbie Laird, Milwaukee General Manager Phil Wittliff and Sherbrooke of the AHL all called to try talking Chin into coming to training camp. He was still disillusioned.

"I never played the game to get to the next level because I never dreamed of going to the NHL," Chin said. "I just loved playing the game, but it wasn't fun any more. It didn't even interest me."

He and Diane were living in Chicago at the time, and Colin spent time relaxing and working out with his former teammates, but when they started to leave for training camp, he began to realize he missed the game. He wasn't ready to get a real job so he reconsidered and called Laird, who had been the most persistent suitor. Chin decided he'd play in Fort Wayne for one year and live with his parents to save money while Diane remained in Chicago working for the university. His first Fort Wayne contract was for $20,000.

``I figured this would be a neat way to bring things full circle and finish up," Chin said.

He came back for one year and ended up staying for 10.

There was plenty of curiosity about the homegrown newcomer whom 99 percent of Komets fans had never seen play – except for one night when he was five years old. During Chin's first exhibition game, Laird started him at center between rugged veterans Dale Baldwin and Steve Salvucci. It was an eventful evening.

``I remember this guy hitting me near the bench and thinking I'm going to have to fight," Chin said. ``This is my hometown, and I'm going to have to fight. I drop my gloves and I was trying to get loose, and I throw a punch and the guy goes down. I'm thinking `Oh, yeah!'"

Except it was Salvucci who had hit the opponent, clobbering him. When that fight was broken up and as the opponent was being escorted to the penalty box, Baldwin jumped in to hand out a few more lumps.

``I'm thinking, `This is good, I like this,' " Chin said. "It kind of set the tone and that was a great year. The game was fun again. I just enjoyed it so much that I figured I'd play another couple of years."

While spending extra time at the rink, Chin learned plenty from Baldwin and Salvucci which shaped the rest of his career as a Komet, especially when he was named captain in 1989. The first Komet team Chin played on was close on and off the ice, and he always tried to recapture that camaraderie.

``I didn't see any of that when I was at Baltimore, but I got a chance to see that at the pro level my first year here," Chin said. ``They had a really good group of guys. That's back when you weren't making a lot of money, and you had guys coming from NHL teams. We were able to keep that going for several years. That's what always made playing a lot of fun."

That closeness helped rekindle Chin's love for the game. Once again he loved being at the rink every day, being around the guys on and off the ice. He was having fun again, and the game wasn't just a job any more.

Chin scored 33 goals and 75 points in 75 games his first season and 31 goals and 66 points in 75 games the next year. His numbers dipped a little in his third Fort Wayne season as Laird asked Chin to concentrate on his defense.

When asked if he felt pressure being the hometown hero, Chin said, ``All 10 years. I think it got more manageable at some point, but when things were going bad, it's tough going home and watching the news and hearing how you sucked or reading in the paper how you sucked, and everybody else hearing that you sucked. I think it got manageable over time, but there was still always pressure. I think the last year and a half when I was hurt, that bothered me the most. I didn't like to think that maybe some people were seeing me for the first time, and I was like that. That's why, when I was done I was done."

After Laird left to join the Washington Capitals, in 1989-90 the Komets named former player-assistant Al Sims the coach and he named Chin his captain. During his final season as a player, Sims said he saw Chin's leadership abilities and knew he'd make a great captain.

"He's a funny guy who cracks guys up all the time," Sims said. "I think his on-ice leadership was probably the biggest thing for him, but he was also extremely good in the room. Not only was he a real rah-rah guy, but he would stand up and say things, but I know if I went in and gave the guys a bunch of crap, he'd break the tension with some comment after I'd left. Guys really respected him for that."

That meant that besides having the pressure of being the hometown hero, Chin was also the team leader and the first one to answer questions when things went poorly. Usually, that worked out very well as the Komets followed Chin's lead and were successful. Sims gave Chin and the other leaders control of the locker room and told them to handle any problems.

``We had the latitude to figure it out and say hey, we're accountable," Chin said. ``I think part of it is because we spent a lot of time together, and people were able to air out their stuff. There was such an environment where there weren't any guys who were showered and gone as soon as practice was over. There was always time to talk and air stuff out because everybody liked being around each other and hanging around all the time."

When the Komets started their great run during the early 1990s, reaching the Turner Cup Finals three times in four years, camaraderie was their main advantage. The Komets won games, Chin said, because the players played for each other and held themselves accountable on and off the ice.

``We won most of those games just because of our locker room," he said. ``There was a time during that stretch where guys on other teams would always shake their heads at us. 'How can they keep beating us?' Players recognized that camaraderie and that atmosphere, because you either have it or you don't. There were a lot of guys who would hear about it by talking to other guys who had played here or friends on the team, and they'd hear what a great place it was to play. There were a lot of guys who were willing to take a little less money to come and play here."

Chin would lead everyone in partying until all hours of the night, but the next morning he'd be in their faces making fun of them if they slacked off during practice. It was somewhat easy for him because he loved being at the rink and around his teammates that much. If they were going to play hard off the ice, they better be prepared to work hard on it.

That closeness led to the Komets' rebirth season in 1990-91 when they surprised everyone by reaching the finals against Peoria. After a great regular season, the run ended too soon the next year, but the Komets rebounded in 1992-93 to shock San Diego in the finals. The Gulls had put together the best season in minor league hockey history before running into the Komets who won all 12 of their playoff games.

``There were a lot of guys there who people didn't think were all that great before that," Chin said. ``They came up with that vagabond thing, but to be honest, we really never rallied around that. It wasn't so much that we believed in ourselves, but everybody knew they were accountable because other guys would hold them accountable. People weren't afraid. It didn't take long for that to sink in."

Maybe the greatest thing about that period was it came during the absolute height of the IHL. It seemed each team had 10 to 15 future NHL players, and the pace of play each night was incredible. The players were also making significant money, meaning they truly were playing in the second-best league in the world.

``Now you're playing against guys you can stack yourself up against," Chin said. ``I remember one year in the mid-90s when there were half a dozen guys who were in the top 10 in scoring in the NHL who had played in the I. At some point you get the satisfaction of knowing, whether I play a game in the NHL or not, I think I could and it really doesn't matter."

Actually, Chin had a chance to sign an NHL contract once. On January 13, 1991, Chin scored four goals and seven points as the Komets destroyed Indianapolis and goaltender Dominik Hasek. After the game, Chin and his father were eating at Wrigley Field when Tampa Bay Lightning executive Tony Esposito approached.

``I didn't come down to look for you, but you're the only one I'd take," Esposito said and offered to sign Chin for the next season.

``Unless you are going to sign me to a one-way, if I'm going to end up in the minors, I'd prefer to stay here," Chin said.

``I was making decent money. Part of my choice to be here was it was fun again, and it was never my dream to play in the NHL. I look back now and think do I wish I would have played one game or a year or two years? That doesn't bother me. And then I think if I had done that, then maybe I'm not sitting here where I am today. It all worked out well. The neat thing about that was my Dad was standing next to me when he said it."

There were a couple of other potential opportunities that didn't work out. Chin was content being one of the best players in the IHL. As the league improved in quality, so did Chin.

``If he was my height, he probably would have played in the NHL and been a household name," long-time teammate Steve Fletcher said. "He had great hands."

His size always seemed like it should have been a detriment, but it never was.

"He was not the biggest guy, not the fastest guy, but he always found ways to get it done," Sims said.

One reason Chin was such a great captain was because he never let his teammates get too high after wins or too low after losses. They could be on a long winning streak, but he never let the celebrations affect the next night's effort. Losses were the same thing.

Maybe the greatest example came during the 1994 playoffs. Compared to the previous three seasons, the Komets struggled during the 1993-94 regular season, but they kept persevering during the playoffs, in part because of Chin's leadership, and a miraculous goal. During Game 6 of the series against Peoria, Chin picked up a loose puck behind the Peoria net, faked left, right and then left again a he tried to elude Rivermen defenseman Jason Marshall. Marshall didn't know where Chin was going so he made a desperate grab for him and missed, which is just what Chin was waiting for.

While Marshall picked himself off the boards, Chin cut toward the Peoria net. Rivermen goaltender David Goverde trying to cut off the angle, but Chin kept skating left, teasing Goverde with the puck. Eventually Goverde fell to his knees and then to his stomach like a fish flopping for air, trying with everything he had to keep his glove up. When Goverde finally went down, Chin gently lifted the puck into the top of the net.

The goal took the heart out of the Rivermen as the Komets won the game to clinch the series. Komets coach Bruce Boudreau said it was ``probably the most beautiful goal I've seen in a decade.''

With Chin leading the way in scoring and leadership, the Komets surprised everyone by making it back to the finals against Atlanta. They probably should have won back-to-back titles but lost a critical Game 4 at home in triple overtime after leading 5-0 in the second period.

Somehow the Komets rebounded to come back and win the next game at home to force a Game 6 in Atlanta. Then the wheels came off. With high-scoring forwards Mitch Messier and Vladimir Tsyplakov injured and unable to play, the Komets were lethargic during the first two periods.

``It's the only thing in hockey I wish I could take back,'' Chin said. ``It was after the second period and we were down by a goal. There was a bunch of water on the table and I came in and took my stick and just smacked everything off the table. I was screaming, `I can't believe we won that last game to come all the way back here, and you guys are just laying down.' There were a few guys I called out.

``It was sickening because it came from nowhere. You could understand if it happened in Game 5, but we had worked so hard to win that game and come back down there. We were already short-handed, and some guys were just lying down. The thing that made me the maddest was if we had worked our hardest and gotten beat, then they were just better than us, but I don't think we even put any offense together. What hurt the most was we were all playing for something and we were letting each other down. I just felt like we had more there. I just couldn't grasp it."

That turned out to be the last of great team achievements during Chin's career with the Komets, though there were still some outstanding individual games.

After scoring a career-high 100 points in 1993-94, Chin came back the next season to get off to a great start with 24 points in the first 22 games, but he was heading up ice on November 26, 1994 in Indianapolis when Ice forward Mike Prokopec stuck his leg out to knock knees with Chin.

``He just caught me," Chin said. ``I remember going down, and I remember rolling around on the ice because I was in pain, and I heard all these people cheering. I'm thinking in my head, what is wrong with you?"

The anterior cruciate and medial collateral ligaments in his right knee were torn, requiring reconstructive surgery. The prognosis was for a rehabilitation lasting eight months to a year, but Chin surprised everyone by making it back in four months to start the first game of the playoffs. Because he wanted to play so badly, Chin was essentially playing on one leg when he could have sat out and no one could have protested. He had another year remaining on a contract and he might have been better served to continue his rehabilitation.

The knee still wasn't fully healed when the 1995-96 season opened, and Chin was limited to 50 games, scoring 31 points. The highlight was playing his 700th career game as a Komet, something only Terry Pembroke, Eddie Long, Len Thornson and Lionel Repka had done. He re-injured his knee, again in Indianapolis on a knee-to-knee hit, this time by Ice defenseman Brad Werenka. He came back from that but later suffered torn ligaments in his thumb.

Despite all the injuries, Chin kept fighting back. In his last great game, with the Komets trailing Orlando 1-0 in Game 3 of the best-of-five first-round playoff series, Chin scored three goals in the final five minutes as the Komets won 3-1. They lost the next two games, including a possible clinching Game 4 in Fort Wayne. The worst part was Chin was stoned by Orlando goaltender Allan Bester in three one-on-one situations during the last game as the Komets lost by one goal.

Chin continued to work out that summer, but the Komets had other plans. After someone from WOWO called late that summer to ask Chin about the Komets not offering him another contract, Chin received a call from Komets General Manager David Franke. The Komets were indeed going another way, and Chin had the option of looking for a contract somewhere else. He felt he should have heard it first from the Komets.

``I was very disappointed, and that kind of stuck with me a little while, probably longer than it should have," Chin said.

Chin ranks fourth on the franchise's career games played list with 746, fifth with 285 goals, seventh with 422 assists and fourth with 707 points. He's also 18th with 638 penalty minutes.

There were offers from Las Vegas and Orlando, but neither included a second year. He never seriously considered taking the offers, but just getting them made the transition to retirement much easier.

``I thought maybe it was just time to go," Chin said. "I realized I didn't have to prove anything to anybody, I only had to prove it to myself. From that standpoint, it made it an easier decision. I thought you know, I'm going to end up back here so does it make sense to leave now and just push that back another year?"

Chin took a job with Lincoln Financial where he's been ever since, now serving as an assistant to a vice president.

For the most part, he's never missed hockey, spending time watching his kids play, first daughter Taylor, who later moved on to volleyball, and now son Cullen who, like his father, is becoming a play-making center.

``There's only been one time where I missed it just a little," Chin said. "I was sitting in the Lincoln box at a game one time, and I didn't miss the game, but they played 'Welcome to the Jungle,' and there was one part of the song that I could feel some goose bumps rising. It wasn't to get out there and play again, but it was like sometimes a smell can remind you of an old girlfriend. It's not that you want to be with her again, but it reminds you."

His No. 26 now hangs from the Memorial Coliseum rafters. Not bad for a player who didn't want to play hockey any more before he came home.

``That's the one thing that playing where it came full circle, knowing I was a part of what the Komets were when I was growing up," Chin said. ``When I look up and see names like Repka, Thornson, Long and… So I'm with those guys? That's pretty neat to even be mentioned with those guys let alone to hang up there with them."

And whatever happened to that No. 1 Spaceman jersey? It's hanging in Cullen's closet.

Colin Chin's career statistics Playing Regular season*Playoffs

Season	Team	League	GP	G	A	PTS	PIM	GP	G	A	PTS	PIM
85-86	Baltimore	AHL	78	17	28	45	38	*	*	*	*	*
86-87	Fort Wayne	IHL	75	33	43	75	35	9	3	1	4	12
87-88	Fort Wayne	IHL	75	31	35	66	60	6	4	0	4	4
88-89	Fort Wayne	IHL	76	21	35	56	71	11	5	4	9	8
89-90	Fort Wayne	IHL	74	21	38	59	79	2	0	2	2	2
90-91	Fort Wayne	IHL	65	18	35	53	69	17	6	6	12	25
91-92	Fort Wayne	IHL	73	35	55	90	64	7	3	6	9	8
92-93	Fort Wayne	IHL	69	30	51	81	44	8	5	2	7	10
93-94	Fort Wayne	IHL	81	36	67	100	71	18	9	10	19	24
94-95	Fort Wayne	IHL	22	10	15	25	10	3	0	0	0	2
95-96	Fort Wayne	IHL	50	11	20	31	36	5	4	1	5	6

CHAPTER 14

FORT WAYNE KOMETS HALL OF FAME

Executive

Ken Ullyot,   1958-82

Colin Lister, 1958-85

Ernie Berg, original owner

Ramon Perry, original owner

Harold Van Orman, original owner

Players

Eddie Long, 1952-66

Len Thornson, 1957-70

Terry Pembroke, 1964-67, 1969-78

Robbie Irons, 1967-81

Chuck Adamson, 1962-67

Merv Dubchak, 1963-70

Reggie Primeau, 1960-69

Lionel Repka, 1958-69

George Drysdale, 1953-55

John Goodwin, 1962-69

Robbie Laird, 1975-79, 1984-86

Roger Maisonneuve, 1958, 1962-66

Cal Purinton, 1963-67, 1968-73

Norm Waslawski, 1958-59, 1962-69

Ted Wright, 1962-70

Bobby Rivard, 1963-66, 1974-75

Terry McDougall, 1975-82

Colin Chin, 1986-96

Steve Fletcher, 1982-83, 1990-96, 2002-03

Coach, trainer

George Polinuk

Marc Boileau

Media

Bud Gallmeier, News-Sentinel

Bob Reid, Journal-Gazette

Carl Weigman, Journal-Gazette

Hilliard Gates, WKJG

Bob Chase, WOWO

Dick DeFay, WKJG

Builders

Don Myers

Dick Zimmerman

Flossie Zimmerman

Earl Stritmatter

Win Rood

CHAPTER 15

WHERE ARE THEY NOW?

(listing of former Komets as of July, 2008)

Aberhart, Bruce * Sarnia, Ontario

Ablett, Jeff * Kimberly, British Columbia

Adam, Russ * St. John's, Newfoundland

Adamson, Chuck * Fort Wayne

Adey, Paul * Coaching in Italy

Aikens, Bert * Rochester, Minnesota

Aimoe, Randy * Gaylord, Michigan

Aitken, Brad * Oshuwa, Ontario

Allison, Dave * Coaching Iowa, AHL

Amadio, Neil * Port Morien, Nova Scotia

Ambroziak, Peter * Rio Rancho, New Mexico

Anderson, John * Coaching Atlanta, NHL

Andres, Bruce * West Vancouver, British Columbia

Arman, Krikor * Ann Arbor, Michigan

Armstrong, Chris * Played in Germany in 2007-08

Atchison, Don * Mayor of Saskatoon, Saskatchewan

Attwell, Bob * Bolton, Ontario

Averill, Steve * Granby, Quebec

Austin, Jon * International Falls, Minnesota

Baker, Ron * Pickering, Ontario

Baker, Ryan * Calgary, Alberta

Bailey, Bob * Deceased

Baillargeon, John * Charlesbourg, Quebec

Baird, Bob * Markham, Ontario

Baird, Jim * Cardston, Alberta

Baldassari, John * Fort Wayne

Baldwin, Dale * Fort Wayne

Balon, Chick * Prince Albert, Saskatchewan

Bancroft, Steve * Madoc, Ontario

Banks, Darren * Pleasant Ridge, Michigan

Bannerman, Murray * Naperville, Illinois

Barahona, Ralph * Lakewood, California

Barlow, Marc * Addison, Ontario

Bartoli, Moe * Deceased

Baryluk, Ron * Brandon, Manitoba

Baseotto, Bruno * Calgary, Alberta

Bashkirov, Andrei * Played with HC MVD in Moscow, Russia in 2007-08

Batherson, Norm * Aylesford, Nova Scotia

Bawa, Rob * Richmond, British Columbia

Beadle, Sandy * Regina, Saskatchewan

Beauregard, David-Alexandre * Played with Tulsa, CHL in 2007-08

Beauregard, Stephane * St. Luc, Quebec

Belanger, Hugo * Played with Mission de Sorel-Tracy, LNAH in 2007-08

Belisle, Ivan * Chilliwack, British Columbia

Bennett, Bill * Cranston, Rhode Island

Berger, Phil * Dearborn, Michigan

Bergland, Tim * Thief River Falls, Minnesota

Bernard, Gary * Peoria, Arizona

Besidowski, Roman * Deceased

Beveridge, Craig * Victoria, British Columbia

Bezeau, Andy * St. John, New Brunswick

Billows, Larry * Winnipeg, Manitoba

Binkley, Les * Hanover, Ontario

Birnie, Scott * Thorold, Ontario

Bishop, Wayne * Richmond Hill, Ontario

Bjorkstrand, Todd * Coaching in Denmark

Black, Ryan * Elmira, Ontario

Blackwood, Bill * North Bay, Ontario

Blaisdell, Wally * Calgary, Alberta

Blaylock, John * Abbottsford, British Columbia

Blondin, Edgar * Deceased

Blondin, Ken * Deceased

Bloom, John * Fort Wayne

Blue, John * Costa Mesa, California

Boguniecki, Eric * Played in Ingolstadt, Germany, 2007-08

Boehm, Rick * Coaching in Germany

Boh, Aaron * Lafayette, Louisiana

Boileau, Marc * Deceased

Boimistruck, Fred * Homepayne, Ontario

Boland, Mike * London, Ontario

Bolduc, Tommy * Played with Quebec Radio X, LNAH in 2007-08

Bonar, Dan * Winnipeg, Manitoba

Bond, Bill * Winnipeg, Manitoba

Bondarev, Igor * Played in Denmark in 2007-08

Boone, Ken * Indianapolis, Indiana

Bouchard, Frederic * Played with Quebec Radio X, LNAH in 2007-08

Bouchard, Robin * Playing with Muskegon, IHL

Boudreau, Bruce * Coaching Washington, NHL

Boudreault, Rene * Kingston, Rhode Island

Boulanger, Gaston * Saint-Boniface, Manitoba

Boulay, Francis * Scheplerville, Ontario

Boulton, Eric * Played with Atlanta, NHL in 2007-08

Boyce, Ian * Fort Wayne

Boyd, Jim * Toronto, Ontario

Bozoian, A.J. * Played with Corpus Christi, CHL in 2007-08

Bradley, Walt * Kitchener, Ontario

Bragagnola, Bob * Timmins, Ontario

Bragnalo, Christian * Faribault, Minnesota

Braumburger, Gus * Huntington, Indiana

Brdarovic, John * Whitby, Ontario

Briere, Michel * Gatineau, Quebec

Brochu, Stephane * Clio, Michigan

Bronilla, Rich * Played in Germany in 2007-08

Broten, Paul * Richfield, Minnesota

Brown, Bob * Vancouver, British Columbia

Brown, Rich * Des Moines, Iowa

Brownlee, Ray * Brandon, Manitoba

Brujic, Damir * Sudbury, Ontario

Brunel, Ray * Winnipeg, Manitoba

Buchanan, Mike * Vancouver, British Columbia

Buchanan, Neil* Toronto, Ontario

Bucyk, Terry * Deceased

Buckley, Mike * Goaltending coach at University of Massachusetts

Bulloch, Nelson * Chicago, Illinois

Burfoot, Scott * Rockford, Illinois

Burgers, Martin * Fort Wayne

Burman, Mike * North Bay, Ontario

Burman, Ron * Decatur, Indiana

Burnette, Barry * Charlotte, N.C.

Bunette, Casey * Whistler, British Columbia

Burnie, Stu * Coldwater, Ontario

Burton, Jim * Evans, Georgia

Busby, Chris * Played with Elmira, ECHL in 2007-08

Butsayev, Viacheslav * Played in Russia in 2007-08

Butters, Mike * General manager of Norfolk, AHL

Byers, Dan * Red Wing, Minnesota

Cabana, Chad * Bonnyville, Alberta

Calder, Eric * Waterloo, Ontario

Caley, Ryan * London, Ontario

Calhoun, Ed * St. Catherines, Ontario

Camazzola, Tony * Barnaby, British Columbia

Cameron, Dave * Mississauga, Ontario

Campbell, Cory * Toronto, Ontario

Campbell, Derek * Played in Newcastle, England in 2007-08

Campbell, Ed * Played with Kalamazoo, IHL in 2007-08

Carlson, Jeff * Muskegon, Michigan

Carmichael, Roy * Dayton, Ohio

Carpentier, David * New York, New York

Cava, Rory * Thunder Bay, Ontario

Cermack, Peter * Bratislava, Slovakia

Cernich, Kord * Anchorage, Alaska

Chabot, Frederic * St. Charles des Drummond, Quebec

Chambers, Shawn * Pequot Lakes, Minnesota

Channel, Craig * Nashville, Tennessee

Channell, Bob * St. Catharines, Ontario

Charbonneau, Stephane * Voorhees. New Jersey

Charko, Wally * Aurora, Ontario

Charron, Craig * Spencerport, New York

Chartier, David * Saskatoon, Saskatchewan

Chaulk, Colin * Played with Komets in 2007-08

Cheveldae, Tim * Moose Jaw, Saskatchewan

Chevrier, Alain * Boca Raton, Florida

Chibirev, Igor * Assistant coach with HC MVD in Moscow, Russia

Chin, Colin * Fort Wayne

Clarke, Mike * Morgantown, West Virginia

Clifford, Chris * Kingston, Ontario

Cole, Mark * Played with Fayetteville, SPHL in 2007-08

Comrie, Fred * Edmonton, Alberta

Conway, Paul * Fort Wayne

Coole, Ryan * Duluth, Minnesota

Coombs, Joe * Dubuque, Iowa

Corbin, Yvan * Anchorage, Alaska

Corpse, Keli * London, Ontario

Correia, Mike * Tewksbury, Massachusetts

Couture, Paul * Livonia, Michigan

Couturier, Sylvain * Bathurst, New Brunswick

Cozzi, Andy * Bellmore, New York

Crawford, Pete * Springfield, Illinois

Creighton, Fred * Sacramento, California

Cronin, Shawn * Boynton Beach, Florida

Crowe, Phil * Scout with Colorado, CHL

Currie, Dan * Burlington, Ontario

Cutts, Don * Toronto, Ontario

Dameworth, Chad * Royal Oak, Michigan

Darling, Dion * Played in Cardiff, England in 2007-08

Davidson, Garry * Salmon Arm, British Columbia

Davidson, Lee * Assistant coach, Minnesota-Duluth

Dearden, Chris * Windsor, Ontario

Debenebet, Nelson * Northville, Michigan

DeCock, Murray * Hamilton, New York

DeGraauw, Corky * Bladel, Netherlands

Delonge, Gary * Deceased

Desjardins, Stephane * Anjou, Quebec

Desjarlais, Craig * Leesburg, Virginia

Dickson, Bob * Ottawa, Ontario

DiMarco, Vic * Toronto, Ontario

Dineen, Jim * Ottawa, Ontario

Dineen, Shawn * Nashville Predators scout

Dobie, John * Regina, Saskatchewan

Doersam, Mike * Cambridge, Ontario

Dolson, Derek * Played with Bloomington, IHL in 2007-08

Dombkiewicz, Mike * Buffalo, New York

Donovan, Rob * Hillsborough, New Jersey

Donnette, Dan * Played in Chuncheon City, South Korea in 2007-08

Doucette, Dave * Yarmouth, Nova Scotia

Doyle, Rob * Lindsay, Ontario

Draper, Tom * Binghamton, New York

Drouin, P.C. * Played with Komets in 2007-08

Drumm, Brian * Orono, Ontario

Drysdale, George * Fort Wayne

Dubchak, Merv * Kenora, Ontario

Duffus, Parris * Fort Wayne

Dufour, Michel * Montmagny, Quebec

Dumas, Claude * Coaching in Telford, England

Dumba, Al * Regina, Saskatchewan

Duncanson, Craig * Sudbury, Ontario

Dunlop, Tim * Midland, Ontario

Dupuis, Marc * Cornwall, Ontario

Eade, Chris * Played with Dayton, ECHL in 2007-08

Eberle, Derek * Regina, Saskatchewan

Blake Sebring

Edwards, Roy * Deceased

Egeland, Tracy * Coach, Rocky Mountain, CHL

Ego, Wayne * Whitby, Ontario

Elcombe, Kelly * Winnipeg, Manitoba

Elynuik, Pat * Calgary, Alberta

Emmons, John * Macomb, Michigan

Endean, Craig * Winston-Salem, North Carolina

Erickson, Dan * Saskatoon, Saskatchewan

Ericson, Leif * New York, New York

Essensa, Bob * Bluffton, South Carolina

Evans, Doug * Peterborough, Ontario

Evans, Shawn * Truro, Nova Scotia

Ewasiuk, Terry * Edmonton, Alberta

Facto, Frank * Deceased

Fahey, Trevor * New Port Richey, Florida

Farrish, Dave * Assistant coach with Anaheim, NHL

Faulkner, Dave * Minneapolis, Minnesota

Ferguson, John * Deceased

Feschuk, Marty * North Battleford, Saskatchewan

Fiebelkorn, Jed * Davie, Florida

Filion, Serge * Quebec City, Quebec

Fillian, Martin * Davenport, Iowa

Findlay, Tim * Windsor, Ontario

Fingerhut, Tim * Richland, New Jersey

Fitchner, Bob * Carman, Manitoba

Fletcher, Steve * Fort Wayne

Fleury, Jerry * Dunedin, Florida

Flichel, Todd * Amherst, Nova Scotia

Fogg, Stan * Deceased

Fowler, Bob * Minneapolis, Minnesota

Franke, Joe * Fort Wayne

Frezell, Skip * Montreal, Quebec

Gaber, Steve * Deceased

Gabrielsen, Jonas * Played in Norway in 2007-08

Gagne, Jacques * Quebec City, Quebec

Gagnon, Dave * Roanoke, Virginia

Gainey, Steve * Kamloops, British Columbia

Galbraith, Lance * Played with Idaho, ECHL in 2007-08

Galipeau, Roger * North Bay, Ontario

Gallant, Gerard * Assistant with New York Islander, NHL

Gallimore, Jamie * Edmonton, Alberta

Garant, Sid * Hendersonville, Nevada

Garvey, Liam * North Chicago, Illinois

Gates, Randy * Cranbrook, British Columbia

Gaudet, Bob * Coach of Dartmouth College

Gaudreault, Mark * Coaching in Switzerland

Gauthier, Derek * Fort Wayne

Gauthier, Sean * Phoenix, Arizona

Gernander, Ken * Warba, Minnesota

Gibb, John * Nobleton, Ontario

Gilhen, Randy * Winnipeg, Manitoba

Gilles, Emile * Roanoke, Indiana

Gilmour, Darryl * Vancouver, Washington

Goodwin, John * Lima, Ohio

Goodwin, Jonathan * Taunton, Massachusetts

Gould, Orrin * Boston, Massachusetts

Goulet, Jason * Warroad, Minnesota

Goverde, David * Orlando, Florida

Graham, Dirk * West Springfield, Massachusetts

Gratz, Brian * Coach of Indiana, MAHL

Gray, Bob * Detroit, Michigan

Grenville, Chris * St. Catharines, Ontario

Gretzky, Brent * Brantford, Ontario

Grills, Chad * Flint, Michigan

Grobins, Nathan * West Palm Beach, Florida

Gruhl, Scott * Richmond, Virginia

Guinn, Rob * Deceased

Gurskis, John * Played with Twin City, SPHL in 2007-08

Halverson, Trevor, Wawa, Ontario

Hamill, Frank * Clifton Park, New York

Hamr, Radek * Played in Switzerland in 2007-08

Handy, Ron * Lafayette, Louisiana

Hankinson, Peter * Edina, Minnesota

Hankinson, Randy * West Branch, Michigan

Hannon, Brian * Houghton, Michigan

Hansis, Ron * Vice President of Hockey Operatins, ACHL

Harding, Jeff * Doylestown, Pennsylvania

Harkins, Todd * North Vancouver, British Columbia

Harrison, George * Deceased

Hart, Art * Deceased

Hartig, John * Port Huron, Michigan

Hartje, Tod * Bloomfield Hills, Michigan

Hawley, Joe * Peterborough, Ontario

Hayes, Garth * Strathmore, Alberta

Hazlett, Steve * Sarnia, Ontario

Heaviland, Tom * Vista, California

Hehir, Bob * Boston, Massachusetts

Herniman, Steve * Muskegon, Michigan

Hextall, Rick * Deceased

Hickey, Greg * Toronto, Ontario

Hicks, Jamey * Timmons, Ontario

Hiltner, Mike * Saint Cloud, Minnesota

Hilworth, John * New Haven, Indiana

Hoganson, Paul * Tucson, Arizona

Holden, Mark * North Ridgeville, Ohio

Holderness, Brian * Saskatoon Saskatchewan

Holland, Dennis * Vernon, British Columbia

Hollett, Steve * St. John's, Newfoundland

Holliday, Kevin * Cochenour, Ontario

Holmes, J.R. * Played with Amarillo, CHL in 2007-08

Honkanen, Jani * Played in Finland in 2007-08

Houlder, Bill * North Bay, Ontario

Horvath, Tony * Hamilton, Ontario

Hrycuik, Jim * Saskatoon, Saskatchewan

Hrynewich, Tim * Muskegon, Michigan

Hudon, Gil * Zenon Park, Saskatchewan

Hueppelheuser, Jason * Lethbridge, Alberta

Hunt, Les * Thunder Bay, Ontario

Hunter, Bart * Calgary, Alberta

Hunter, Matt * Edmonton, Alberta

Hurd, Kelly * Fort Wayne

Hynek, Dave * Oakville, Ontario

Imoo, Dusty * Vancouver, British Columbia

Ing, Peter * Niagara Falls, Ontario

Irons, Robbie * Fort Wayne

Jago, Paul * Mount Dennis, Ontario

Jakubo, Mike * Sudbury, Ontario

Janaszak, Steve * Babylon, New York

Janecyk, Bob * Ottawa Senators scout

Jarram, John * Kitchener, Ontario

Jay, Bobby * Scottsdale, Arizona

Jennings, Grant * Anchorage, Alaska

Jensen, Darren * Kelwona, British Columbia

Jensen, David * Minneapolis, Minnesota

Jerrard, Paul * Assistant with Iowa, AHL

Johnson, Darcy * Yorkton, Saskatchewan

Johnson, Norm * Portland, Oregon

Johnston, Doug * New Haven, Indiana

Johnston, Jay * West Lafayette, Indiana

Jones, Bob * Sault Ste Marie, Ontario

Jones, Brad * Assistant commissioner of IHL

Jorde, Ryan * Played with Flint, IHL in 2007-08

Joyal, Lou * Winnipeg, Manitoba

Joyce, Duane * Pembroke, Massachusettes

Kaminski, Kevin * Coaching Youngstown, CHL

Kampurri, Hannu * Helsinki, Finland

Karalis, Tom * Muskegon, Michigan

Kardash, Mike * Deceased

Kastelic, Ed * Phoenix, Arizona

Kastelic, Joe * Muskegon, Michigan

Kean, Jason * New York, New York

Kearns, Justin * Sylvania, Ohio

Keates, Brian * Deceased

Keating, D'Arcy * Sault St. Marie, Ontario

Keissig, Brant * Thunder Bay, Ontario

Keller, Ralph * Humelstown, Pennsylvania

Kenny, Matt * Belleville, Ontario

Kenny, Shane * Fort McMurray, Alberta

Kenny, Shane * Fort McMurray, Alberta

Keough, Jim * Plymouth, Michigan

Kernahan, Jack * Deceased

Kerr, Kevin * Coaching Flint, IHL

Keyes, Richard * Kalamazoo, Michigan

Kiessig, Brant * Thunder Bay, Ontario

Kikendall, Ed * Indianapolis, Indiana

Kirk, Bob * Oshawa, Ontario

Kirton, Scott * London, Ontario

Kiyaga, Arthur * Played with Tulsa, CHL in 2007-08

Knickle, Rick * Scout with Nashville, NHL

Kobezda, Jan * Ilava, Slovakia

Kobylarz, Paul * Jonkoping, Sweden

Kocur, Kory * Edson, Alberta

Kolenda, Mike * Grand Rapids, Michigan

Kollman, Tony * Drumheller, Alberta

Kostenko, Greg * Maple Ridge, British Columbia

Kotsopoulos, George * Fort Wayne

Kotyluk, Kevin * Boston, Massachusetts

Krivokhija, Yuri * Squirrel Hill, Pennsylvania

Krueckl, Tim * New Rochelle, New York

Kulyk, Glenn * Duluth, Minnesota

Kuntar, Les * Ocala, Florida

Kurk, Kevin * Orchard Park, New York

Labarre, J.F. * Played with Trois Riviere, LNAH in 2007-08

LaBelle, Don * Knoxville, Tennessee

Labrecque, Patrick * Innsbruck, Austria

Lackner, Andrew * Played with Tulsa, CHL in 2007-08

LaForest, Bob * Welland, Ontario

LaGrand, Scott * Director of Player Personnel, Charlotte, ECHL

Laird, Robbie * Fort Wayne

Lakso, Bob * Orr, Minnesota

Lallo, Moose * Pampano Beach, Florida

Lalonde, Bobby * Pickering, Ontario

Lambert, Dan * Played in Germany in 2007-08

Lambert, Judd * Richmond, British Columbia

Lampshire, Ian * Vancouver, British Columbia

Landman, Erik * Heerenveen, Netherlands

Lane, Gord * Columbia, Maryland

Laniel, Marc * Oshuwa, Ontario

Lanthier, Michael * Montreal, Quebec

LaPlante, Sebastien * Moncton, New Brunswick

LaPointe, Norm * Laval, Quebec

Laverdiere, Justin * Woonsocket, Rhode Island

Laurin, Steve * Barrie, Quebec

Lawrence, Doug * Tulsa, Oklahoma

Lawson, Tom * Played in Russia in 2007-08

Layzell, Brad * Geneva, Illinois

LeBlanc, John * Campbelton, Manitoba

LeBlanc, Ray * Largo, Florida

LeCompte, Eric * Played in Italy in 2007-08

Leef, Ron * Fort Wayne

Legge, Randy * Newmarket, Ontario

Lehtera, Tero * Nummela, Finland

Lekun, Mike * Sudbury, Ontario

Lemay, Dave * Thunder Bay, Ontario

Leslie, Bob * Pilot Mound, Manitoba

Letourneau, Glenn * Minnetonka, Minnesota

Letzgus, Steve * Port Huron, Michigan

Levie, Craig * Calgary, Alberta

Lewis, Adam * Fort Wayne

Lindsay, Mark * Kelowna, British Columbia

Llano, Kirk * Montreal, Quebec

Loach, Lonnie * St. Peters, Missouri

Lockett, Ken * Oakville, Ontario

Loder, Jeff * St. John's, Newfoundland

Lomow, Byron * New Haven, Indiana

Long, Eddie * Fort Wayne

Longmuir, Colin * Vancouver, British Columbia

Loustel, Ron * Winnipeg, Manitoba

Lowdermilk, Dwayne * Langley, British Columbia

Lowe, Steve * Byron Center, Michigan

Lubiniecki, Darryl * Prince George, British Columbia

Lucas, Corey * Buffalo, New York

Luciuk, Andrew * Prince George, British Columbia

Lucyk, Carey * Fort Wayne

Lunny, Joe * Boston, Massachusetts

MacDonald, Aaron * Red Deer, Alberta

MacDonald, Kevin * Bakersfield, California

MacDonald, Todd * Taylor Mills, Kentucky

MacDougall, Kim * Regina, Saskatchewan

MacGuigan, Bob * Charlottetown, Prince Edward Island

MacMillan, Jeff * Played in Manchester, England in 2007-08

MacNeill, Bernie * Murillo, Ontario

MacPherson, Forbes * Assistant coach with Texas, CHL in 2007-08

MacPherson, Murray "Muzz" * Deceased

Madigan, Con * Portland, Oregon

Magliarditi, Marc * Las Vegas, Nevada

Maisonneuve, Roger * Deceased

Maillett, Claude * St. Joseph's, New Brunswick

Major, Bruce * Topsfield, Massachusetts

Malarchuk, Garth * Grande Prairie, Alberta

Mallet, Kurt * Exeter, New Hampshire

Maltais, Steve * Dollard des Ormeaux, Quebec

Malykhin, Igor * Fort Wayne

Mancini, Paul * Erie, Pennsylvania

Manganaro, Sal * Toronto, Ontario

Marini, Hector * Mississaugua, Ontario

Marshall, Bobby * North York, Ontario

Marshall, Terry * Rapid City, Manitoba

Martens, Darren * Mossback, Saskatchewan

Martin, Craig * Amherst, Nova Scotia

Martin, Mike * Grand Bend, Ontario

Mason, Bob * Goaltending coach for Minnesota Wild

Massie, Michel * Played with Mission de Sorel-Tracy, LNAH in 2007-08

Mastad, Milt * Wood Mountain, Saskatchewan

Masters, Tyler * Coaching at Bowling Green in 2007-08

Matechuk, Rod * Abbotsford, B.C.

Matter, Trevor * Leduc, Alberta

Maxfield, Lloyd * Marysville, Michigan

May, Darrell * Chilliwack, British Columbia

Mayes, David * Thunder Bay, Ontario

McAllister, Kyle * Played in ECHL in 2007-08

McBain, Andrew * Toronto, Ontario

McBride, Dean * Deceased

McCaig, Doug * Deceased

McCallum, Dunc * Deceased

McCauley, Wes * NHL referee

McCloskey, Kevin * Fort Lauderdale, Florida

McCord, Dennis * Deceased

McCusker, Bob * Port Coquitlam, British Columbia

McDougall, Terry * Flint, Michigan

McFall, Dan * South Burlington, Vermont

McKee, Brian * Fort Wayne

McKercher, Jeff * Toronto, Canada

McLeod, Hartley * Deceased

McMichael, Scott * Deceased

McNaught, Bill * Orlando, Florida

McNiece, Bob * New Westminster, British Columbia

McNeill, Bob * Stoufeville, Ontario

McNeill, Mike * Granger, Indiana

McQueen, Barry * Winnipeg, Manitoba

McRae, Chris * Beaverton, Ontario

McVie, Tommy * Boston Bruins scout

Meier, Ron * Saskatoon, Saskatchewan

Melanchuk, Shorty * Deceased

Melichar, Jan * Played 2006-07 in England

Melson, Taj * Plymouth, Minnesota

Messier, Mitch * White Lake, Michigan

Metzger, Ben * Pickering, Ontario

Mezin, Andrei * Played in Russia in 2007-08

Middendorf, Max * Scottsdale, Arizona

Miehm, Kevin * Whitby, Ontario

Milam, Jamie * Played with Gwinnett, ECHL in 2007-08

Miller, Bob * Kitscoty, Alberta

Miller, Keith * Indianapolis, Indiana

Miller, Kelly * Played with Wheeling, ECHL, in 2007-08

Millette, Robert * Coaching in France

Milne, Andy * Sudbury, Ontario

Minor, Gerry * San Diego, California

Minor, Jim * Vancouver, British Columbia

Mitchell, Bill * Perrysburg, Ohio

Mokosak, Carl * Comstock Park, Michigan

Molin, Sacha * Stockholm, Sweden

Molleken, Lorne * Saskatoon, Saskatchewan

Morency, Pascal * Played with Bridgeport, AHL in 2007-08

Morin, Vic * Hearst, Ontario

Morrow, Dave * Sherwood Park, Alberta

Motz, Rob * Alliston, Ontario

Mulvenna, Glenn * Flager Beach, Florida

Murphy, Rob * Stittsville, Quebec

Murray, Rob * Assistant with Providence, AHL

Natyshak, Mike * Toledo, Ohio

Naumenko, Gregg * Lincolnwood, Illinois

Nelson, Tom * Stoughton, Wisconsin

Nemeth, Tom * West Milton, Ohio

Nemirovsky, David * Played in Russia in 2007-08

Nemirovsky, Mikhail * Played in Germany in 2007-08

Neumeier, Troy * Played in Belfast, Ireland in 2007-08

Newans, Chris * Anchorage, Alaska

Neziol, Tom * Deceased

Nikolic, Alex * Carp, Ontario

Nikulin, Igor * Westminster, California

Nordstrom, Carlin * New Battleford, Saskatchewan

Norris, Dave * Unionville, Ontario

Nowicki, Todd * Buffalo, New York

O'Brien, Earl * Deceased

O'Driscoll, Dan * Jacksonville, Florida

O'Neill, Mike * Chicago, Illinois

Oksiuta, Roman * Retired in Russia

Oleschuk, Bill * Calgary, Alberta

Olsen, Ian * Agassiz, British Columbia

Olson, Eddie * Deceased

Orban, Bill * Saskatoon, Saskatchewan

Ortmeyer, Jake * Played 2007-08 with Bossier-Shreveport, CHL

Ostlund, Lowell * Saskatoon, Saskatchewan

Ostlund, Stu * Vancouver, British Columbia

Pagnutti, Rick * Sudbury, Ontario

Pajor, Greg * Simcoe, Ontario

Park, Jim * Thornhill, Ontario

Parker, George * Regina, Saskatchewan

Parrish, Dwight * Coaching in England

Parrish, Geno * Played with Corpus Christi, CHL in 2007-08

Parro, Dave * Hershey, Pennsylvania

Parsons, Steve * Calgary, Alberta

Patenaude, Rusty * Williams Lake, British Columbia

Patten, Erik * Wolfeboro, New Hampshire

Pearson, Jim * Tilbury, Ontario

Pederson, Tom * Los Gatos, California

Pembroke, Terry * LaGrange, Texas

Penasse, Mike * Barre, Ontario

Penn, Shawn * Madison Heights, Michigan

Pentland, Dwayne * Penticton, British Columbia

Pepin, RIchard * Montreal, Quebec

Perkins, Don * Indianapolis, Indiana

Perna, Mike * St. Catharine's, Ontario

Perrault, Kelly * Tipp City, Ohio

Pesetti, Ron * Laval, Quebec

Petrakov, Andrei * Played in Russia in 2007-08

Phillips, Bob * Indianapolis, Indiana

Pilling, Gregg * Edmonton, Alberta

Pinfold, Dennis * Edmonton, Alberta

Piro, Josh * Played with Fayetteville, SPHL in 2007-08

Pizunski, Ed * Muskegon, Michigan

Plante, Cam * Brandon, Manitoba

Polinuk, George * LaOtto, Indiana

Poliziani, Dan * Mansfield, Massachusetts

Pooley, Paul * Notre Dame assistant coach

Pooley, Perry * Dublin, Ohio

Popp, Kevin * MacNutt, Saskatchewan

er, Dale * Toronto, Ontario

Pozzo, Gary * Calgary, Alberta

Prediger, Ivan * Edmonton, Alberta

Prestage, Wayne * Bashaw, Alberta

Price, Dan * Toledo, Ohio

Primeau, Reg * Fort Wayne

Purdie, Brad * Played in Austria in 2007-08

Purinton, Cal * Sicamous, British Columbia

Purves, John * Ottawa, Ontario

Pye, Bill * Saginaw, Michigan

Quinn, Mike * Lewiston, New York

Racine, Bruce * Troy, Missouri

Ramsay, Bruce * Coached Muskegon, IHL in 2007-08

Ramsay, Glenn * Toledo, Ohio

Randall, Bruce * Thunder Bay, Ontario

Randall, Gerry * Fort Wayne

Randolph, Mike * Duluth, Minnesota

Rankin, Jack * Chicago, Illinois

Ratushny, Dan * Nepean, Ontario

Ray, Derek * Fort Wayne

Raymond, Alain * Rimouski, Quebec

Reddick, Eldon (Pokey) * Henderson, Nevada

Reid, Doug * Fort Erie, Ontario

Reid, Shawn * Denver, Colorado

Reincke, Terry * Fort Wayne

Reirden, Todd * Assitant coach Bowling Green in 2007-08

Ricciardi, Gary * Bourbannais, Illinois

Richard, Jean-Marc * Pont-Rouge, Ontario

Richardson, Billy * Fort Wayne

Richardson, Bruce * Played with Wichita, CHL in 2007-08

Richardson, Dave * Winnipeg, Manitoba

Richison, Grant * Fort Wayne

Rideout, Scott * Mankato, Minnesota

Rigler, Doug * Fort Wayne

Rioux, Gerry * Iroquois Falls, Ontario

Rissling, Kelly * Edmonton, Alberta

Rivard, Bob * Peterborough, Ontario

Robert, Claude * Deceased

Rodberg, Steve * Twig, Minnesota

Rohlicek, Jeff * Saskatoon, Saskatchewan

Romaniuk, Russ * Winnipeg, Manitoba

Ronson, Len * Gresham, Oregon

Ronan, Dan * Boston, Massachusetts

Ross, Dave * Calgary, Alberta

Rouleau, Mike * Sault Ste Marie, Ontario

Rowland, Chris * Portland, Oregon

Roy, Andre * Played with Tampa Bay, NHL in 2007-08

Roy, Serge * Sept-Iles, Quebec

Rubachuk, Brad * Calgary, Alberta

Rudenko, Bogdan * Asheville, N.C.

Rumble, Brent * Coquitlam, British Columbia

Rupp, Duane * Delmont, Pennsylvania

Rycroft, Al * Penticton, British Columbia

Ryder, Dan * Chicago, Illinois

St. Croix, Rick * Winnipeg, Manitoba

St. John, Jimi * Windsor, Ontario

St. Pierre, Kevin * Played with Tulsa, CHL in 2007-08

Sachl, Petr * Played in Czech Republic in 2007-08

Salvain, Dave * Burlington, Ontario

Salvucci, Mark * Derry, New Hampshire

Salvucci, Steve * Plymouth, Massachusetts

Sanscartier, Dan * Quebec City, Quebec

Savage, Joel * Zug, Switzerland

Savoia, Ryan * Played in Italy in 2007-08

Schmidt, Kevin * Bloomington, Indiana

Schofield, Dwight * Fairview Heights, Illinois

Schreiber, Wally * Fort Saskatchewan, Alberta

Scully, Barry * Bobcaygeon, Ontario

Selleke, Jason * Played in Italy in 2007-08

Selmser, Sean * Played in Austria in 2007-08

Seney, Scott * Silver Springs, Maryland

Severson, Ryan * Carlos, Minnesota

Sewell, Joey * Calgary, Alberta

Shantz, Brian * San Antonio, Texas

Sharapov, Vadim * Moscow, Russia

Shargorodsky, Oleg * Farmington Hills, Michigan

Shaunessy, Scott * Duxbury, Massachusetts

Shaw, Jim * Saskatoon, Saskatchewan

Shelstad, Brad * Wadena, Minnesota

Sheremeta, Dean * Moonbeam, Ontario

Sheridan, John * Minneapolis, Minnesota

Shields, Kelly * Played in Yugoslavia in 2007-08

Shires, Jim * Trabuco Canyon, California

Shmyr, Brian * Vancouver, British Columbia

Shmyr, Paul * Deceased

Shoebottom, Bruce * Boston, Massachusetts

Short, Bill * Calgary, Alberta

Shudra, Ron * Sheffield, England

Shulmistra, RIchard * Apex, North Carolina

Sidorkiewicz, Peter * Head coach of Erie, Pennsylvania, OHL

Siemon, Jack * Deceased

Sikich, Zach * Played in 2007-08 in China

Sillers, Gerry * Vancouver, British Columbia

Simchuk, Konstantin * Played in Russia in 2007-08

Simpson, Shawn * Toronto Maple Leafs scout

Slota, Kevin * London, Ontario

Slukynsky, Fred * Sault Ste. Marie, Ontario

Smith, Darin * Vineland, Ontario

Smith, Dave * Coaching Canisius College

Smith, Mark * Played in Italy in 2007-08

Soccio, Len * Hanover, Germany

Soetaert, Gary * Saint Albert, Alberta

Sonier, Grant * Scout with Boston, NHL

Sprott, Jim * Oakville, Ontario

Stajduhar, Nick * Kitchener, Ontario

Stanutz, George * Deceased

Stas, Sergei * Played in Belarus in 2007-08

Staub, Bill * Winnipeg, Manitoba

Stefan, Joe * Assistant with Plymouth, OHL

Stevens, Bart * Mason, Ohio

Stewart, Blake * Played with Bloomington, IHL in 2007-08

Stewart, Bobby * Toronto, Ontario

Stewart, Danny * Played with Coventry, England in 2007-08

Stewart, Glenn * Assistant coach at University of Connecticut in 2007-08

Stone, Art * Virginia Beach, Virginia

Strasser, Paul * Sebringville, Ontario

Strueby, Todd * Regina, Saskatchewan

Summerfield, Garrett * Huntsville, Alabama

Sutcliffe, Eric * Cranbrook, British Columbia

Sutton, Boyd * Solodtna, Alaska

Sutyla, Ken * Winnipeg, Manitoba

Swain, Garry * West Simsbury, Connecticut

Swain, Matt * Oakville, Ontario

Syroczynski, Matt * Played with Elmira, ECHL in 2007-08

Tabaracci, Rick * Park City, Utah

Talotti, George * Spokane, Washington

Tataryn, Josh * Played in the Netherlands in 2007-08

Tebbutt, Greg * North Vancouver, British Columbia

Teskey, Doug * Toledo, Ohio

Therrien, Jean * Quebec City, Quebec

Thomson, Floyd * Dunchurch, Ontario

Thomson, Terry * Edmonton

Thornson, Len * Fort Wayne

Tiley, Brad * Played in Austria in 2007-08

Timmins, Jack * Deceased

Tippett, Brad * Regina, Saskatchewan

Toffolo, Mark * St. Louis, Missouri

Tok, Chris * Assistant at Michigan Tech

Tomalty, Glenn * Calgary, Alberta

Tomlinson, Kirk * Halifax, Nova Scotia

Tompkins, Dan * Minneapolis, Minnesota

Toner, Glenn * Ottawa, Ontario

Torchetti, John * Assistant coach with Chicago, NHL

Torchia, Mike * Kitchener, Ontario

Tosh, Brian * Ottawa, Ontario

Townsend, Andy * Monroe, Connecticut

Tremblay, Erick * Played with Wichita, CHL in 2007-08

Tretowicz, David * Liverpool, New York

Tsulygin, Nicholai * Played in Russia in 2007-08

Tsyplakov, Vladimir * Assistant coach with Belarus National Team

Tudor, Rob * Okotoks, Saskatchewan

Turner, Mark * Tecumseh, Ontario

Tuzzolino, Nick * Played with Flint, UHL in 2007-08

Twordik, Brad * Brandon, Manitoba

Uhlrich, Rick * Toronto, Ontario

Ulanov, Igor * Played in Russia in 2007-08

Ullyot, Ken * Fort Wayne

Ullyot, Ron * Apopka, Florida

VanderBreggen, Josh * Milton, Ontario

Vani, Carmine * Coaching in Italy

Venedam, Sean * Bakersfield, California

Veysey, Sid * Bedford, Nova Scotia

Vichorek, Mark * Cloquet, Minnesota

Virag, Dustin * Fort Wayne

Voorhies, K.J. * Knoxville, Tennessee

Voykin, Andy * Deceased

Walby, Steffon * Coach of Mississippi, ECHL

Walker, Brian * Beaver Lodge, Alberta

Walmsley, Ivan * Richmond Hill, Ontario

Walter, Brett * Gibbons, Alberta

Ward, Lance * Played in Sweden in 2007-08

Waslawski, Norm * Fort Wayne

Watson, Billy * Deceased

Weekes, Kevin * Played with New Jersey, NHL in 2007-08

Weingartner, Rob * Coaching Wichita, CHL in 2007-08

Welker, Billy * Shreveport, Louisiana

Wells, Mark * St. Claire Shores, Michigan

Wetzel, Carl * Gaylord, Minnesota

Wharton, Len * Deceased

White, Alton * Surrey, British Columbia

White, Scott * General manager with Iowa, AHL

Whiteside, Cy * Colorado Springs, Colorado

Whyte, Noah * Toledo, Ohio

Wickenheiser, Doug * Deceased

Wiggins, Mike * Calgary, Alberta

Wilcox, Jim * Nepean, Ontario

Wilkes, Bill * Regina, Saskatchewan

Wilkie, Bob * Palmyra, Pennsylvania

Willard, Rod * Wilbraham, Massachusettes

Willett, Paul * Bakersfield, California

Wilson, Jim * Deceased

Wilson, Pat * Deceased

Wilson, Rik * St. Louis, Missouri

Wilson, Ross * Washington, Michigan

Wilson, Steve * St. Louis, Missouri

Winnes, Chris * Warwick, Rhode Island

Wood, Derek * Prince George, British Columbia

Woods, Bob * Coached Hershey, AHL in 2007-08

Worlton, Jeff * Bradford, Ontario

Wortman, Kevin * Lynn, Massachusetts

Wright, Ted * The Villages, Florida

Wright, Chris * Fort Wayne

Wynn, Rick * Fort Wayne

Wywrot, Pete * Seattle, Washington

Yakubov, Ravil * Moscow, Russia

Yashin, Oleg * Voskresensk, Russia

Young, Gary * Calgary, Alberta

Zanier, Reno * Trail, British Columbia

Zanussi, Ron * Rossland, British Columbia

ABOUT THE AUTHOR

Blake Sebring has been a sportswriter for the Fort Wayne, Indiana, News-Sentinel for 25 years and has covered the Fort Wayne Komets for nearly 20 seasons. "Legends of the Komets" is his second book on the team following ``Tales of the Komets" in 2006. He is also co-author of "The Biggest Mistake I Never Made" with Olympic volleyball gold medalist Lloy Ball and ``Live from Radio Rinkside: The Bob Chase story." He hopes to publish the novel "The Lake Effect" in the near future.

Printed in the United States
136284LV00003B/2/P